THE MANKIND SERIES OF GREAT ADVENTURES OF HISTORY

Great Military Campaigns

THE MANKIND SERIES OF GREAT ADVENTURES OF HISTORY

Great Military Campaigns

Compiled, edited and with an Introduction
by Raymond Friday Locke

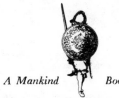

A Mankind   *Book*

MANKIND PUBLISHING COMPANY
LOS ANGELES

Book design by Andrew Furr.

CONTRIBUTORS

Albert E. Cowdrey taught history at Tulane, Newcomb and Louisiana State University before retiring from the academic world to write. His novel, *Elixir of Life,* was recently published by Doubleday.

Angela Stuart, a free lance writer living in Los Angeles, has published articles in both scholarly and popular journals. Nancy Anderson, the West Coast editor of a national magazine, specializes in the history of England and Scotland.

Richard L. Blanco is, an associate professor of history at the State University College of Brockport, Brockport, New York.

Charles E. Adelsen has lived in Turkey for almost a decade and recently completed a book on the people and republic of Turkey.

William F. Lewis, a former Fulbright Fellow in Spain, teaches history at the University of California, Santa Barbara.

Ake Sandler, professor of political science at California State College, Los Angeles, is the son of the former Foreign Minister of Sweden, Richard Sandler. He has published textbooks in both America and Sweden.

INTRODUCTION

"War is hell," said the American Civil War general, William Tecumseh Sherman, and war is particularly hell for the losers. This collection of articles on great military campaigns of history concentrates, to a great extent, on the unsung heroes of losing causes. Among the "losers" profiled in this collection are Xavier Mina, who became a Spanish national hero by leading a force of guerrillas against Napoleon during the Peninsular Campaign of 1808-1814 and lost his life, as so many other Europeans have done, by involving himself in Mexican politics; Tyrone of Ulster, who led the Irish of his day in their war for independence from the British; Boabdil of Granada, who lost Moorish Spain to the Christians; Marshal Mannerheim, who gallantly led the Finnish army against the Russian invasion of 1939; Bonnie Prince Charlie, who led a rebel force against the British crown; and Dowager Empress Tzu Hsi, who lost her throne as a result of the Boxer Rebellion.

What can we learn from reading military history? I once wrote, "The object of history is not only to understand the past; it is to understand the present by looking at the past." Certainly, in a time when world military powers are capable of destroying the world by the push of a button, these words should apply to military history. I say *should* for it seems, to date, that we have learned very little by studying man's past military mistakes.

RAYMOND FRIDAY LOCKE
Editor, Mankind Magazine

Mehmet II outside Constantinople

CONSTANTINOPLE: THE LAST BATTLE OF EAST ROME

By Albert E. Cowdrey

*E*urope was threatened from the East, Christian statesmen called vainly for unity in a divided West, and a great capital stood isolated behind the lines of the advancing Eastern power. Not an unfamiliar situation; surely we read about it in the headlines of the day before yesterday. Yet it all happened five hundred years ago, and the city in question, unlike its modern analogue, was allowed to perish. And that is the more remarkable because Constantinople in 1453 meant far more to western Europe than Berlin ever has. The heir both of Greece and the Eastern Roman Empire, Constantinople had preserved the law and classics of the ancient world through the Dark Ages until the West was again able to understand and use them. Nor was the city only a capital of the spirit. Its walls had shielded Europe for a thousand years against every threat from the East, Moslem and pagan, down to the time of the Ottoman Turks.

At first the Ottomans had seemed no different from the others. One of the clans of central Asia which had suffered defeat at the hands of Genghis Khan, the Ottomans had drifted down into the Anatolian plain and overrun the Seljuk Turks who prevailed there. Inevitably, they had taken up the Seljuks' ancient quarrel with the Byzantine Empire, whose eastern lands the Seljuks had been unjointing and devouring since the eleventh century.

To the newcomers the Empire presented itself as a greatly weakened and hugely tempting prize. Stripped of its dominions in the east, the city on the Bosphorus was at odds with its possible allies in the west. The old schism between Greek and Latin, Orthodox and Catholic, went unhealed in the fifteenth century despite the labors of the Council of Florence. The capture and looting of Constantinople by western "crusaders" two hundred years before had never been forgotten or forgiven by the Greeks. And the Papacy—which had once been able to summon all Europe to the Crusades—was itself weakened and declining, absorbed by the wars of Italy, and increasingly slighted or ignored by the emerging powers of Europe. Each in its own way, Rome and Constantinople were passing into the shades.

In the mid-fifteenth century, no one could have foreseen that the landmarks of the medieval world were falling astern quite so swiftly. The young pushing nations of Europe knew well enough, however, that the Empire was a venerable ghost, and its death was contemplated with a good deal of resignation.

The Turks waxed strong on the division and indifference of the West. Under a succession of gifted sultans, they entered Greece itself, and conquered it from the Peloponnesus to the borders of Hungary. They further carried the battle across the Danube and, under the

Sultan Murad, defeated the hero John Hunyadi at Varna and Kossovo, on the "Plain of Blackbirds."

When the last of the Greek Emperors, Constantine Paleogogue (Constantine XI), was crowned at Mistra in the Morea, in January, 1449, the empire once ruled by Constantinople had shrunk to the city itself and a hundred miles or so of fields and vineyards beyond the walls, and the Peloponnesus. Divided from the West by the presence of the Turks, from western sympathy by an old schism and a new secularism, divided by time from its own past when it had power and glory and meaning in the scheme of things, the city faced its youthful enemies almost alone.

The vigor of the newcomers was particularly attested when a new sultan succeeded Murad in 1451. Only twenty-two, the man who was Mehmet II (Mohammed, in Arabic) was a powerful and arresting figure: handsome, cruel, hardened by the intrigues of his father's court and the life of a military people, he was also given to philosophy and he dreamed of gaining a reputation that would place him beside Alexander as a conqueror of men.

For this reason the city obsessed him: an insomniac, he brooded night after night over the plans of its defenses; his days were spent in reviewing his immense military forces, in questioning spies, and in receiving diplomats, including those of the Greeks. To the latter he was particularly kind, swearing "by God and His Prophet, by the angels and the Koran," that he would observe the treaties of peace that they had signed with his father.

He waited just about a year before making the first move. Early in 1452 a Turkish army arrived on the shore of the Bosphorus, opposite the great Asiatic fortress of Anatoli Hissar. The countryside was methodically plundered, lime kilns were set up, and a Turkish fleet arrived from the Dardanelles to protect the laborers, who soon arrived on the scene, and to ferry materials from Asia. While the Greeks protested, a great fortress began to rise on the European shore—the castle Roumili Hissar, which, with its grim sister across the waves, would control the Bosphorus by its cannonfire. Soon Constantinople would be shut off from the Black Sea ports, the source of its grain supply.

For the first time the methods and demonic energy of the young sultan were put on view. Both were dismaying. Five thousand skilled workers, each with two apprentices, were moved en masse to the site of the castle. The "labor problem" was solved with extreme simplicity: each mason was ordered to build an arm's breadth of wall every day, or his head would be cut off. Fearing to seem idle, even the highest personages of the Turkish empire pitched into the work, hauling mortar and stones at the direction of lowly masons.

Meantime, flying squads of cavalry scoured the countryside, foraging supplies and sending slaves to work at the fortress. Villages which resisted were burned, treated to massacres, and left in ashes with a few impaled bodies to draw flies. The work went on.

In August, 1452, Roumili Hissar stood complete—a triangle of walls and towers twenty to thirty-six feet thick, armed with cannon that fired stone balls weighing six hundred pounds. The Bosphorus, a Greek or Roman sea since Homeric times, was commanded wholly by Turkish guns.

Alarmed by the reports of the frenzied villagers who poured into the city from the ravaged countryside, the Emperor ordered the gates of Constantinople to be closed against possible attack. Toward the end of August, the Greeks standing watch on the walls were treated to a remarkable spectacle. On his way home from Roumili to his capital at Adrianople, Mehmet with an army of fifty thousand men stopped off to look over the field of future operations.

He studied the topography first-hand, ostentatiously and at leisure, for three days. Then he moved on, to be received at his capital with wild enthusiasm by a people who already coupled the word "Conqueror" (Fatih Sultan Mehmet) with his name. He spent the winter in completing his preparations for the siege of the Queen City.

It was a winter of labor, warfare, and anguish. The Peloponnesus was invaded and the Greek despots who ruled there were shut up in their fortresses; Arcadia was ravaged; to the north, every town and tower that might hinder an army was carried by assault. Constantinople, meanwhile, was shaken by supernatural terrors. A perfect hailstorm of portents battered the city: the earth rumbled, strange lights were reported in the sky, wandering stars appeared and vanished, and icons bled or wept or vanished from their niches like soldiers taking plow-furlough.

But the Emperor Constantine showed himself a ruler, to the surprise of some. A man of no special talents, middle-aged, childless, in all ways the opposite of his brilliant enemy, he proved able to make the most of his moderate gifts: laborious, devoted, a settler of differences, able to inspire in a quiet way, he led his city, with its reduced population, its mixture of races and creeds, to the complex and exhausting labor of defense.

The walls were repaired; thousands of tombstones from adjacent graveyards were embedded in their fabric; monasteries were forced to give up their treasures; Europe and Asia were scoured for provisions; weapons were bought and made, and emissaries were dispatched to plead for help from the West. Also, quietly, and against the embittered opposition of the people and the monks, Constantine began to move toward a new union with the Roman Church. Westerners resident in the city—mainly Venetians and Genoans—were brought by the monarch's quiet persuasiveness and the logic of

13

their own peril to take an active part in the work of defense.

Spring came—the year was 1453—and the almond trees began to bloom behind the walls. Under the guard of Turkish soldiers, huge cannon groaned into sight, dragged by ox-teams over the Thracian plain. And in March, the great army of the Turks arrived en masse.

How big was that army? Nobody knows although the estimates run up to 250,000 men. That it was huge no one disputes. The heart of the great host was the Turkish feudal levies, summoned from the whole empire; these were sturdy troops, armed in mail, carrying shields, helmets, scimitars, lances, and bows. Finest of the fighting men assembled were the fifteen thousand Janissaries, professional household troops of the sultan, kidnapped as children from Christian families and raised as Moslems and soldiers.

Uncounted "bashi-bazouks" followed the army, an irregular rabble made up of both Moslems and Europeans, all drawn by the hope of spoil. They were ill-armed, with light shields or "targets," a scimitar, and no body armor except a leather jerkin quilted with cotton to slow missiles. Such were the soldiers.

Also present were imams and dervishes, drawn by the *jihad*, the holy war against the unbelievers; European craftsmen and artillerymen from Serbia, Germany, Hungary, and western Europe; swarms of peddlers and merchants, cutthroats and rogues of every sort; slaves, servants, and women camp-followers; religious fanatics dreaming of heaven in the fumes of hemp; and, to complete the picture, herds of cattle and goats, flocks of domestic fowl, sheep and dogs, mules and horses and camels—the whole family of Ottoman on the move, with all that it possessed. Like a vast cloud of seabirds, screeching and quarreling, shedding feathers and droppings, the army began to settle and

A Janissarie. The Janissaries were Christian allies of Mehmet II.

roost before the walls.

As they settled, the cannon began to speak. The largest of the Turkish bombards was twenty-six feet long, with a bore of thirty inches; its stone ball weighed twelve hundred pounds. This monster, named the "Royal" according to the custom of the day, was mounted just out of bowshot in the valley of the river Lycus, which flowed under the walls and through the city to the sea of Marmara. The ancient walls of Theodosius, bleached and weathered pink and gold by a thousand years, shuddered and cracked at the first impact of the huge stones.

These walls were Europe's ancient cuirass. The inner wall had been constructed by Theodosius and strengthened by Heraclius. It was forty feet high, crenelated, with massive towers sixty feet tall. It was, for lack of men, unoccupied during the siege; the fighting went on along the lower barriers and in the "parabolas," or open spaces separating the walls.

The outer wall was twenty-five feet high, with towers rising twice that; and a low stone breastwork ran along the fosse, or ditch, which was flooded in parts and dry in others. Within the walls were blooming orchards, palaces, and the cemeteries whose headstones had been plucked out during the winter's repair operations. Plane trees, cypress, almonds, both wild and domestic, and pomegranates grew near the walls. Cattle grazed, and fenced gardens turned green as vegetables fattened in the warm spring weather. An Elysian scene —except for the clouds of dust drifting back from the stricken walls; the reeking powder smoke, the massive reverberations of the cannon.

To take advantage of the damage done by the "Royal," Mehmet had pitched his pavilion in the Lycus valley and commanded that part of the line himself. There, too, the Janissaries made their camp. To the Grand Turk's right, the Anatolian levies under Isaac

Pasha held the ground to the Sea of Marmara; to his left, the bashi-bazouks and European levies, to the land-locked Golden Horn; while north of the Horn, occupying Pera and watching the Genoese settlement of Galata, Zagan Pasha with some forty thousand men completed the circuit of the landward walls.

The Greeks had raised a boom and a massive chain to block the entrance of the Horn, and the warships of the Greeks and their Western—mainly Venetian—allies, were drawn up behind the chain. While northward off the Bosphorus coast, at a spot called Two Columns, the Turkish fleet of 350 vessels was moored in readiness to attack the chain and defending fleet whenever the army should assault the walls.

Within, the forces available to the defense were absurdly small: some eight thousand men in all, counting both Greeks and Italians. John Giustiniani, a Genoese soldier of fortune, was given command of the walls in the Lycus valley, while the Emperor Constantine commanded a tiny reserve force.

Besides the fighting men, the people of the city—who numbered, at this time, probably no more than forty thousand souls—were available for the incessant labor of repairing the walls. The labor of these meager forces was endless and exhausting. All day the Turkish cannons tumbled the threefold walls into wide skirts of rubble, and the Janissaries skirmished beyond the ditch. All night the exhausted soldiers, aided by monks and priests, the old people and women and children of the city, labored to build makeshift barriers of wood, earth, and brush, and cover them with hides against the Turkish incendiaries—burning arrows and grenades of sulphur and naphtha.

Their work was of some use; not only were the gaps in the walls filled, but the barricades of wood and earth proved better adapted to absorb and bury the cannon-balls than the brittle fabric of the original walls.

Against these improvised barriers the Turks brought a fantastic array of weapons: the great bombards, arquebuses, firelock muskets; crossbows, catapults, trebuchets, all the medieval weapons worked by counterweights and twisted rope; and the swords, arrows, lances, and javelins that men had been using during millenia of war. On this battlefield several great strata in the evolution of war were, as if by some inept archaeologist, mixed indiscriminately together.

However armed, the Turks quickly proved themselves heroic and relentless antagonists. While the cannon fired overhead, the infantry skirmished close to the wall, indifferent to the shots of the defenders, watching always for a chance to scale some unguarded area, and scouring the ramparts continually with their arrows.

As the days passed, the pace of the fighting stepped up. On the eighteenth of April, Mehmet ordered an assault in the Lycus valley, where the "Royal" and its attendants had already leveled a long section of the walls. The assault was made at night, but the Turks lost the advantages surprise and darkness might have given them because of their shouting and their use of tambourines and drums to signal their troops. Portions of the barricades were set on fire, and the light enabled the Italians to fire more accurately into the crowded masses struggling in the fosse. After three or four hours of fighting the attack was beaten off.

The very next day, probing at the other extremity of the city, the Turkish fleet attacked the chain guarding the mouth of the Golden Horn. The fighting here was mostly done with missiles, and the efforts of the Turks to break the chain failed. So, the first serious collisions ended with the status quo roughly restored; but immediately afterward came a Christian victory.

One of the chief props for the morale of the defenders was the belief that help would ultimately arrive from the west. The Papacy was believed to be conciliated by Constantine's policy of renewing the union of the churches; Venice was at war with the Turks and had promised a fleet to help the defenders.

All these hopes seemed to be turning into facts when—a day or two after the battle at the chain—four ships hove into sight of the city's walls. Three were Genoese, one Imperial; and they drove straight for the shelter of the Golden Horn, with a strong following wind to give them hopes of reaching it in safety.

Mehmet, as soon as his lookouts reported the sails, galloped to Two Columns and ordered his fleet, which was commanded by a Bulgar renegade named Baltoglou, to capture the newcomers. A hundred and fifty Turkish ships of every description immediately set out, longoared triremes mixed with smaller vessels which were, in a sense, the bashi-bazouks of the fleet.

The strong, heavy ships of the Christians, with their high fo'castles and poops, rammed and smashed the first vessels to attack them, and seemed about to gain the Horn and safety. But then the south wind failed; suddenly becalmed, the Christians floated on subsiding waters, which brought them gradually under the walls of Galata. The Genoese on the walls looked on in horror, unable to help them for fear of breaking their own precarious truce with the Turks. Apparently the ships were doomed.

But the sailors came up with a brilliant tour de force. They bound their vessels together with hawsers, creating a strange floating castle, which drifted across the mouth of the Horn in the absolute calm. The naval fight became a battle of fortification and assault, the sailing ships playing the part of the fortress, upon which the Turks, with high courage but little wisdom, proceeded to rush in wildest disorder. Their galleys crowded together, breaking one another's oars, tangling the rigging.

Meantime, armed cap-a-pie, the Christians beat back

every effort to board their vessels. Thirty or so of the defenders and several hundred Moslems died in the fighting, most of the latter by drowning in their armor. About sundown the south wind wilfully sprang up again, activating the Christian ships, and they cut loose from one another and smashed out of the Turkish fleet, leaving behind them broken ships, floating bodies, and —watching from the shore—ecstatic Christians and an enraged sultan.

Poor Baltoglou had to face his ruler the next day. Pointing to an eye he had lost in the combat (to a mis-aimed Turkish arrow: a good symbol of the battle) he tried to excuse his failure on the grounds of a valiant effort. At first determined to cut off the Bulgar's head, Mehmet moderated his rage a little. Still, he had his admiral thrown on the ground and bastinadoed, de-prived him of his offices, and seized all his possessions to give to the Janissaries. One-eyed now, and sore-boned as well no doubt, Baltoglou was dismissed from history.

The fortunes of the Turks were at their lowest point; repulsed everywhere, they had now been humiliated by a mere handful of Christian sailors. How could Mehmet break the stalemate and retrieve the initiative? The young sultan's answer startled and bemused the world.

It seemed plain that the Turkish fleet, despite its numbers, could not enter the Golden Horn by the front door. Yet it must get in. Even if it did nothing, once in-side the harbor it would compel the Christians to man the walls there also, stretching their meager strength to the utmost. The sultan concluded that if his fleet could not get past the chain and its guardians, it could enter the Horn only one way. He must sail it overland.

Wooden ways were rapidly constructed from the an-chorage at Two Columns, over the heights of Pera, and down to the Golden Horn. Wooden rollers, placed be-tween the ways, would bear the weight of the ships.

Reenactment of the Battle of East Rome

Drawn by men and animals, the ships rose one by one to the top of Pera's vine-clad ridge, and then, as the hawsers were paid out, descended the other side and floated free in the waters of the Horn. From the walls of Constantinople the defenders looked on, stupefied, as some eighty-seven rigged, masted, and armed ships sailed grandly down a hillside, through a sea of vines.

The boats were manned as well, for the Turks, delighting in the incongruity, took their places at the oars and "rowed," while crowds swarmed along beside the ships, striking tambourines, blowing trumpets, hurrahing and shouting as if at a picnic. As the first ship floated free—it was a "fuste," a small war vessel sent ahead to test the ways—the last was rising from the Bosphorus beyond the hills. So, on the twenty-third of April, the "inner sea" was reached by the Turks, the defensive labors of the Christians infinitely extended and worsened, and—more important still—the emperor of the Greeks was brought, apparently for the first time, to despair.

An emissary waited on the sultan, offering on behalf of Constantine a huge yearly tribute in return for peace. Mehmet in turn offered him the despotism of the Morea, under Turkish suzerainty, offices for his brothers, and safety for the people of the city if it surrendered. Otherwise the city would be given to the torch, the people to the soldiers. "I will have Constantinople, even if it is empty of life."

Constantine rejected the offer. As regards the people of the city, the sultan's offer was certainly cynical. Who could have protected them, once the Turkish army was inside the walls? On the other hand, the customs of the day did not demand the supreme sacrifice from a monarch, which makes the emperor's decision to accept the fate of his city the more impressive.

And that fate was now all but certain. Fourteen miles of walls had to be watched night and day; other-

wise a small party might enter the vast city unper-
ceived, overpower the guard at some minor gate, and
open the way to the besieging army. As a final point,
the Turks built a pontoon bridge across the upper
waters of the Golden Horn, to permit the forces in Pera
to join those outside the Theodosian walls at short
notice.

So the daily schedule of incessant bombardment,
skirmishing, alarums, feints, and arrow-play resumed.
Food began to run short inside the walls. All night
long, while the exhausted soldiers dozed in their stink-
ing armor, triumphant cries, drums, cymbals, and trumpets sounded from the Turkish camp, threatening—and
sometimes signaling—attack.

On the night of the sixth of May there were heavy
assaults at widely scattered points, aimed to disperse
the defenders and overwhelm some single point. Guis-
tiniani narrowly escaped death; the chroniclers reported that the Greeks, Italians, and Turks fought together
"like beasts."

On the twelfth a great assault was staged against the
palace of the Porphyrogeneti, at the northern end of the
Theodosian walls. Again the Turks were beaten off, but
not until they had twice penetrated into the streets of
the city, where the emperor himself, rounding up
stragglers and adding them to his small reserve force,
drove them out. Losses on both sides were great.

Above and even beneath the earth the tempo quick-
ened. Mines were run beneath the city's walls, with the
aim of storing gunpowder there and blowing up the
barrier. Fourteen such attempts were made in all, and
all failed. Listening, running countermines, the Christians penetrated the tunnels, sometimes flooding them
with water from the river Lycus, sometimes filling them
with poisonous fumes from naphtha "grenades," sometimes turning them into Dantesque burning tombs with
Greek fire, sometimes fighting the sappers hand to

hand, yards down in the earth.

All in one night the Turks built a great wooden tower in the Lycus valley to overtop the wall and shoot down on the defenders; ferocious assaults and counter-assaults raged around the tower all day, and at night the great structure caught fire from the missiles and naphtha and gunpowder stored inside it, and burned to the ground. Turkish failures above and below the earth left the sultan raging once again: "If thirty-seven thousand prophets had told me this could be, I would not have believed them!"

Clearly events were shaping up to some sort of climactic final struggle. The Christians were exhausted and strained to the utmost to defend the long walls, but the walls had nowhere been entered. The immense army of the Turks could not be held together indefinitely, and there were rumors of a Venetian relief fleet, held up by contrary winds. Every device of siege warfare had failed. The last weapon of the Turks must be the same as the first: men and cannon against walls.

On the twenty-sixth a council of war was held in the Turkish camp. Khalil Pasha, the grand vizier, who had been in treasonable contact with the Greeks, urged that Constantine's renewed offer of an immense tribute should be accepted. But the other notables—the Grand Eunuch, the Zagan and Isaac Pasha, who commanded the wings of the army—all favored a final effort. The sultan quietly checked the feel of the army, found impatience and enthusiasm high, and, in the face of many setbacks, a desperate resolve. The mercurial temper of the troops might not hold. Mehmet declared for an immediate assault.

Furious preparations began at once. Bombards were moved from other sectors to the valley of the Lycus. Every unit was assigned its own duty in the attack; the assault was to be continuous, weary units retiring, fresh troops taking their place, until the city fell. Engines and ladders were prepared, and every blade was turned against a whetstone.

The night of Sunday, May 27, 1453, hardly existed in the Turkish camp. Fires roared all night long, and great waves of cheering followed the repeated reading of Mehmet's proclamation of the assault. The sultan promised all the people and all the riches of the city to the troops. They were to be allowed three days of pillage, without interference—so he promised, on the soul of his father, the heads of his children, and his sword. The uproar was incessant.

Meantime the great bombards were never silent. The "Royal," repaired and returned to service after cracking under its own concussion, was again hurling half-ton boulders at the shattered wall. Every time one struck, says a chronicler, the whole wall shook, buildings in the city shuddered and cracked, even ships rocked uneasily in the waters of the Golden Horn.

The fleet's new admiral received his own orders. The seawalls of the Marmara, the Bosphorus, and the Horn were to be attacked simultaneously with the movement against the Theodosian wall.

One ceremony remained: the harangue, without which no army of those times felt itself fully prepared for battle. On the night of the twenty-eighth, while the Turkish army, under orders, rested around dimmed campfires, Mehmet assembled his officers and Janissaries before his tent.

He spoke of the riches of the city, of the gold and silver and jewels to be found in the churches and palaces, of the wealthy men to be ransomed, of the lovely women and handsome boys to be had by the conquerors. Then he showed that the conquest of the city was ordained by Heaven, and had been foretold by the Prophet. He urged courage and obedience to orders, threatened the most terrible punishment upon slackers and cowards, and declared that the extinction of a

25

thousand-year empire and the most glorious victory of all time was in the offing.

That same night, in the silence that was so striking and portentous after the uproar of the one preceding, the Christians likewise prepared themselves for the final struggle. The Venetian bailey (leader of the Italian colony in Constantinople), the emperor, and the great lords, and all the people of the city moved in procession, bearing wonder-working icons to the ruined wall, and chanting the Kyrie Eleison.

The chief soldiers, senators, and lords of the empire gathered to hear Constantine urge them to fight well, depending on God and the aid of Christ, and to bear themselves as the heirs of Greece and Rome should. He thanked the Italians for their great services, and urged them to stand beside him at the supreme moment.

Then in a profoundly medieval scene, the leaders of the Christians confessed their sins to one another, and begged forgiveness for their own part in past quarrels. Lords and commoners crowded into Haghia Sophia, Justinian's great church, to pray and receive communion. Grimy soldiers, beggars, and Italian soldiers of fortune rubbed elbows with the nobility of the Greeks and the last senators of East Rome. Gradually the great church emptied as the fighting men returned to the walls. No Christian service has been held there since that night.

By now it was past midnight. The emperor rode the circuit of the walls again, inspecting every gate and tower. About two o'clock, hearing a strange, tumultuous murmur, he dismounted and climbed a tower near the Porphyrogeneti Palace. The Turks were moving everywhere, carrying forward ladders and arquebuses, roped and hooked lances, moving in assault columns down from Pera to cross the floating bridge and attack the corner where the Theodosian walls met the seawall along the Golden Horn. The fleet in the Horn was all astir, oars being shipped, decks faintly resounding in the darkness. At the same time, watchers on the southern seawall were discovering that the Sea of Marmara was covered with ships.

In the valley of the Lycus the attack began about three. Fifty thousand bashi-bazouks carrying ten thousand ladders swarmed into the fosse, crying, "There is no god but God!" The Christians, singing the Kyrie Eleison, waited for them atop the heap of rubble, fenced with palisades and wooden breastworks and makeshift crenelations made with barrels of earth. More than a thousand feet of outer wall were down, and, to encourage the troops, the officers had locked the gates of the inner wall: the defenders fought without a chance of escape. They met the bashi-bazouks with a rain of stones, javelins, arrows, bullets, and Greek fire. The irregulars hesitated, and turned to flee. But household troops, armed with maces and lead-weighted whips, were advancing behind them, to lash them on to the assault. Time after time the helpless mob was driven against the Christians, exhausting the defenders, absorbing their weapons. After two hours or so, the remnants were permitted to retire. In the first dimness of the morning, the Anatolians advanced and the real work began.

The Turks flung ladders against the palisades and were hurled down with their ladders into the fosse. They rushed forward in solid waves, and the defenders' guns plowed and harrowed their massed ranks. Mehmet had ordered the bombards to advance during the night; now, suddenly, he ordered them to fire into the struggling masses at the palisade. At point blank range the twelve hundred pound stones demolished the wooden walls, the Greeks, Turks—everything. The new breach was full of drifting smoke, dust, and fragments. The incredible Turks charged into the burning wreckage again. The Christians met them, struggled "body to body, all entangled," and thrust them out once more. On the corpse-littered slope the Turks hesitated. The second wave had failed.

Now Mehmet himself gathered his reserves, his archers, slingers, and musketeers and above all his Janissaries, and led them in person to the fosse. He ordered the archers to cover the remnants of the palisade with an incessant fire, so that no defender could show his head without losing it. Then he ordered the Janissaries to attack and they came on—said an Italian who fought that day, with open admiration—"like lions, roaring; you could have heard them in Anatolia." The best the Turks had was now committed at the palisade. For the third time the struggle was renewed.

The final events took place in a haze of dust and recrimination. Nobody is quite sure how the Turks succeeded. But the story seems to turn about a tiny and forgotten postern toward the north end of the wall, near the Porphyrogeneti Palace. It was called the *Kerkoporta,* the circus gate.

Apparently, under the pressure of attacks raging elsewhere, the defenders left unguarded a relatively undamaged section of the wall. A party of Turks discovered the fact, and, prowling about under the wall came upon the postern and forced it open. Inside they found themselves in the city itself, for the inner wall came to an end near the palace. Mounting a transverse wall, some of the Turks displayed their banners and began to shout that the city had fallen.

Was this fatal? It is hard to say. Most of the Turks who entered the city simply started looting and forgot the battle. But at the Lycus another event took place at about the same time which began a moral collapse among the defenders. John Giustiniani, the Italian soldier of fortune, was wounded in the chest by a canonball. Crying that the wound was serious (in fact it proved mortal) he produced a key to one of the locked

A portion of the Roman Wall of Theodosius

gates in the inner wall, and, ignoring the pleas of Constantine, ordered his followers to carry him to his ship.

His men, already shaken by the appearance of the Turkish banner on the wall, panicked in their leader's absence. They seemed suddenly to have realized that the open gate behind them was their only means of escape if the Turks really were in the city; and by ones and twos, and then, suddenly despairing, in a scuffling mob, they struggled to get through the narrow gate. Heroes of a moment before turned in one second to cowards who fled wailing like women and calling on God to save them. A trickle of men running toward the ships became a brisk river, then a torrent.

Mehmet, seeing the commotion on the palisade, cried to his men, "We have the city!" and he led them in the final scaling of the ruined barricade. Backed against their own inner wall, torn between the need to fight and the desperate desire to escape, the Greeks were massacred. Constantine, exclaiming, "The city is taken, and still I live!" rushed into the thick of the fighting and was slain, perhaps by a Janissary. It was just dawn: six o'clock on the 29th of May.

So the death agony began. At first the Janissaries, annoyed by the stout defense and the long siege, massacred everyone. But then cooler thoughts prevailed, and the Turks returned to their traditional wisdom, "Kill the old, sell the young." The aged, the sick, and the unsalable were butchered; pregnant women and children at the breast, who could not stand the transportation to market, were likewise killed. Severed heads, said an Italian, floated in the Horn "like melons in the canals of Venice."

The young, the handsome, and the rich survived. Herded together, stripped naked, systematically raped and sodomized, the survivors were bound with their own girdles, with priests' stoles, with the bridles of horses and camels, and driven down to be packed into the waiting ships. For those who could not be ransomed, the prison ships and the auction block were a natural destination.

Yet even these were lucky, in a sense, for, following the Janissaries, the bashi-bazouks poured into the city. These were the dregs of two worlds, and the defenders had bled them very industriously a few hours before, and now they were condemned to take the leavings of the Janissaries, and scavenge where the Turks had looted. So the lines of captives owned and guarded by some watchful soldier might take comfort at least in being preserved from the irregulars, who tortured the living wounded and led men through the streets by halters of their own intestines.

The loss in art, in manuscript, was as vast as the loss of life—worse, perhaps, than after the sack by the Crusaders two hundred years before. The accumulations of a millennium, Greek, Roman, Byzantine, were dispersed in a day. The whole precious library was obliterated; volumes of Plato were used to start fires, or sold for a few pence, or thrown into the streets to be walked upon. Ships were ballasted with ancient manuscripts, and precious icons were destroyed for their "idolatry." So the saints, the protectors of the city, perished with the people they had failed. This was the end of Byzantium, the extinction of the last temporal heir of Rome.

On the third day after the fall of the city the sultan visited his new domain and moved with his suite into the scarred and desolated Palace of Blachernes. Walking through the soiled and echoing rooms, he repeated, according to his theatrical nature, a Persian verse: "Today the spider is the guardian of the emperors' palace and spins her web before the gate. The owl wakes the echoes of the royal tomb of Afrasiab with his mournful chant."

Visiting Haghia Sophia, he found a busy fanatic at

work breaking up the floor of the temple, and drove him off with his sword. Then the sultan prostrated himself and cast dust upon his head, in recognition that the empire of the Turks would likewise pass away. A muezzin climbed into the pulpit, all bowed to Mecca, and for the first time the Muslim call to prayer was heard in the ancient Christian sanctuary.

It was time for a lenitive spirit, and Mehmet generally followed a sound policy of reconciliation. Owners of Greek slaves were required to pay them a daily wage, so that they might redeem their freedom. Artisans and merchants were moved into the city from other parts of the Turkish domain. Toleration for the Christian religion was proclaimed.

A contentious monk, Gennadius, whose opposition to the union with Rome had been a perpetual source of trouble to Constantine, was sought out by Mehmet (he had become the slave of a pasha) and made the new patriarch of Constantinople. In his younger days this Gennadius had been a noted Aristotelian scholar, and Mehmet, pursuing his inquiries into the nature of things, liked to summon the patriarch to the seraglio late at night to pass his insomniac hours in discussions of causation, the entelechy, the true nature of the good, and the existence or nonexistence of God.

So the eastern portal of Europe became the Sublime Porte. Where Plato had taught, the Turk settled. The Parthenon at Athens became first a mosque, then to its own misfortune a storehouse of gunpowder. For nearly four hundred years Greece passed out of history. Crusades against the Turk were preached in vain. The new secular powers of the west played the game of power with the Grand Turk, hardly remembering that he was an unbeliever, except when he threatened their own domains.

The seal of Mehmet II

The last council of Boabdil at the Alhambra

BOABDIL, SULTAN OF GRANADA

By John McBride

*T*hese are the keys to the last relics of the Arab Empire in Spain; thine, O Sire, are our trophies, our kingdom and our person. Such is the will of Allah. Receive them with the clemency thou hast promised, and which we look for at thy hands."

With these words Mohammed Abu Abdullah, known as Boabdil El Chico, surrendered the Kingdom of Granada to Ferdinand and Isabel on January 2, 1492, bringing to a close over 780 years of Islamic power in Spain. The fall of the last Moorish Citadel drew the final curtain on almost a millenium of splendor and achievement, which the Arab world has never forgotten and which left an indelible impression on the people and culture of the Iberian Peninsula.

Two women witnessed the young Sultan's humiliation, both of whom were instrumental in bringing about his downfall, albeit in very different ways. At the head of the Christian armies stood Isabel, Queen of Castile and the unrelenting spirit of the *Reconquista*. Elation, pride, and pity were interwoven in her emotions. In truth, *"El Rey Chico,"* the Young King because he had been crowned so early, was as much a victim of Castilian artifice as he was of the ruthless struggles within the Moorish royal family. More than protocol prompted her to call him "our little brother," for the blond, blue-eyed Boabdil was the 25th sovereign in the 260-year reign of the Nasrid kings of Granada. Of remote Arab origin, he, like most of Spain's Moorish rulers, had more Gothic genes than half the Castilian nobility. Boabdil had as much right to call himself Spanish as did Isabel, who had an English grandmother, or Ferdinand, who was part Jewish.

The other woman seethed with bitterness. Sultana Aixa had exerted every wile to secure the throne of Granada for her son, but the final battle had been won by the hated Infidels.

After the initial exchange of amenities, Ferdinand handed the keys of Granada to Isabel. She passed them on to the Count of Tendilla who had already been named governor of the capital. Solicitous to the last, Ferdinand took the Sultan's arm and said, "Come with me to Valladolid. You will be treated like my own brother."

"El Rey Chico" had been stung by the king's brotherly affection too often, however. Taking leave of the Catholic sovereigns he set out for the Valley of Purchena in the wild Alpujarras with his frail wife Moraima, his little son Abdullah, the haughty Aixa, and a retinue of followers. Ferdinand and Isabel had been generous in the surrender terms and, among other concessions, they set aside land in the Alpujarras for the deposed ruler *"para siempre y siempre,"* forever and ever. Legend has it that before entering the mountains,

Boabdil looked tearfully back at Granada for the last time and Aixa, unable to control her fury, spat, "Thou dost well to weep like a woman for that which thou has not defended like a man."

To say that Boabdil did not defend Granada gallantly, in view of the circumstances, would be an insult to historical truth, but, while earnest and just, he was also disorganized and indecisive. His mother was a woman of masculine spirit and he basked in her shadow. Had she not been bound by rigid Muslim tradition, Aixa might have emerged the equal of Isabel. It was the indomitable Aixa who protected the youthful Boabdil from the intrigues of her rival, the Sultana Zoraya, a beauteous blonde of Christian origin who coveted the throne for her own sons, and in manhood Boabdil was rarely out of sight of his mother's touch or the promptings of her will. In truth, Aixa was motivated not only by jealousy and ambition but by genuine maternal affection as well, for a pall of doom hung over Boabdil since birth when the court astrologers foretold that Granada would fall during his reign. Consequently his father, the fierce Muley Abul Hassan, loathed the boy.

Boabdil had neither the tenacity of his mother nor the resolute command of his father. He was a vapid ploy in Aixa's political intrigues and a dupe in the hands of King Ferdinand. Perhaps more than anything else he was a victim of fate—that fate which chose him to be the ruler of the last remnant of an empire that had gradually crumbled before the Christian Reconquest and which was never beyond the shadow of the Cross. Perhaps the Arab chroniclers captured the essence of Boabdil's character best in calling him "El Zoboybi," the Unfortunate One.

Boabdil could well weep at the loss of his domain, for in its way Granada was a microcosm of the Islamic Empire in Spain at its height. The splendor was tarnished but it still glittered. In his chronicle of the wars of Granada, Washington Irving caught the affection of the Moors for *"Al Andalus"* as they called it, Land of the Vandals, when he wrote, "So beautiful was the earth, so pure the air, and so serene the sky of this delicious region, that the Moors imagined the paradise of their Prophet to be situated in that part of heaven which overhung the kingdom of Granada."

With a total population of three million, the Moorish kingdom stretched along the Mediterranean from Gibraltar to Almeria and its capital nestled in the lap of the Sierra Nevada like a bright jewel. The city of Granada was crowned by the Alhambra, the ornate "Crimson Fortress" which still inspires Arab poets to sing its praises as the realization of a Koranic dream. The kingdom contained 14 cities, 97 fortresses and countless unwalled towns and villages.

The Moors were master horticulturists. Fruit-laden vineyards dotted the countryside and the plains shimmered with wheat. The *suks* of the capital overflowed with fine textiles and metal work, and the *Alcaiceria,* silk market, drew merchants from Florence to India. The Nasrid kings cultivated the arts and intellectuals thronged the court, following the footsteps of Averroes, Avenzoar, Ibn Hazm, and all the other illustrious figures who brought glory to Islamic Spain when Cordova was the heart of the Caliphate and rivaled Baghdad as capital of the Muslim world. Granada's Madraza was a major seat of learning and the Arab intellectual fire which brought light to Iberia when Europe was floundering in the Dark Ages still flickered in *"Al Andalus."*

Ibn-al-Khatib, the Moorish physician, called the capital the "Spanish Damascus" and spoke of its architectural wonders, the chivalry of its knights, and the beauty of its women. The Moors led in the development of medical science and, while lepers were being burned and the insane chained in many parts of Europe, Granada had separate hospitals for these unfortunates. The Muslims valued the hygienic properties of water and created public baths called *hamams* far beyond the imagination of their Roman originators. The Christians believed baths to be physically enervating, however, and promptly destroyed them after the Reconquest.

Granada's musical fests called *zambras* united Moor, Jew, and Christian alike in revelry, dancing and singing to a unique hybrid music which would one day emerge as Flamenco. In the Alhambra and the *alcayars*, Moorish aristocracy enjoyed concerts of *Andaloussiyat Muwashah*, the school of Arab-Andalusian music which still retains a major place in Islamic musicology.

But all was not splendor. Poverty was rife and beggars and thieves roamed the streets. Granada itself contained numerous walled quarters and from time to time the inhabitants of the various *barrios* sallied forth to war on one another, until order was restored by the sultan's troops. Marmol, the 16th century chronicler, writes, "The houses of this city were built so close together in Moorish times and the streets were so narrow that there was no more than an arm's breadth between the windows across the street and there were many quarters where horsemen carrying lances could not penetrate."

Architectural clutter had always been endemic to the city, however, for Granada supposedly derived its name from the pomegranate, since when viewed from afar it resembled the cluster of seeds within the fruit. But the name most likely hails from the Arabic *Garnatha Alyehud*, Hill of the Jews, descendants of the 40,000 families brought from Palestine by the Emperor Hadrian. At the time of the Moorish conquest, they made up the majority of the populace. In time the name of the city was applied by the Castilians to the entire region.

Granada bulged with 200,000 inhabitants, equal to

Queen Isabella

the city's present population. Included were a myriad of peoples as well as thousands of Muslim refugees who had fled the Spanish dominions where they were known as *Mudejares*. There were *Mozarabes,* Christians who were "almost Arab" in everything save religion, true Arabs, Syrians, Yemenites, Egyptians, Berbers, Jews, Persians, Turks, and even Hindus. The vast majority in both the capital and the kingdom, however, were *Muladies*, descendants of Spanish converts to Islam, mixed with the early conquerors. There were countless Christian and numerous Negro slaves and some of the Moors had "Slavic" ancestry, tracing their lineage to eastern European slaves who were brought in by the early caliphs as a buffer against Arab-Berber dissension.

At various stages in the peninsula's history these diverse peoples lived in harmony or strife. The Shiah and Sunni sect feuds were rekindled in Spain, Arabs despised Berbers, and the Muslims fought bitterly among themselves as well as with their Christian enemies. And while the Jews achieved their "Golden Age" in Islamic Spain, reaching a pinnacle of intellectual and commercial attainment, they were frequently victims of Muslim pogroms as well as Christian oppression.

With his blondness, sensitivity, and lack of warlike fanaticism, Boabdil typified a dominant type among the Spanish Moors. Although he could trace his ancestry to the illustrious Arab lord Abu Abd Allah Mohammed Ibn 'L-Ahmar, founder of the Nasrid dynasty, the Semitic strain had been diluted through intermarriage with Spanish women. The Moors preferred the blondes of Spain's northern provinces and soon the Celtic-Visigoth strain dominated Moorish ruling families and Galician actually emerged as the *lingua franca* of the harem and court.

The rapid assimilation of the invaders can be readily explained when it is remembered that the "true Mus-

lims" had always been numerically scant. Tarik initiated the conquest in 711 A.D. with only 12,000 Berbers
and Syrians and subsequent invasions were made by
forces of comparatively small numbers. The conquest
was achieved with miraculous ease for various reasons,
principally because of the tyranny and weaknesses of
Spain's Visigoth rulers. The Moors, most of whom were
Berbers, brought few women with them and, in keeping with Islamic custom, took wives and concubines
from among the conquered. They won many converts,
and since they carried with them a basically superior
culture they imposed their rule with comparative ease.
Islamic philosophy had preceded them into Iberia, and
Spain had been oriented to the East since the days of
Phoenecia and Carthage.

Doubtless because the impulse that sparked the Reconquest was Gothic, originating with the first defeat
of the Moors at Covadonga by Pelayo in 718 A.D.,
Spanish Christians often exaggerated their blond features on the one hand and the duskiness of some Moors
on the other, a factor heightened by Moorish rulers
who dyed their beards black in emulation of their distant Arab forebears. Complicating the ethnic puzzle
were the Berbers, a Caucasian people who have inha-
bited North Africa from antiquity and who were themselves converted to Islam by Arab conquerors. Frequently they were blond and blue-eyed; some were of
dark Hamitic strain, aquiline featured, with swarthy
skins and tight curly hair. Most, however, were identi-
cal with the lithe, dark-haired, olive-complexioned
Iberians, the basic racial stock of Spain and Portugal.
Indeed, the ancient Iberians migrated to the peninsula
from North Africa. It was from one of the principal
Berber tribes—the Mauri—that the Spanish derived
the word Moor, a convenient appellation they applied
to all Muslims.

Apart from forced conversions initiated by both

sides, there was a remarkable amount of intermarriage. Many Christian rulers affected Arab dress. They sent their sons to study at the Muslim universities of Cordova, Seville, and Saragossa and gave their daughters in wedlock to Moorish princes. The Sultan of Seville gave his daughter as concubine to his mortal enemy, Sancho of Castile. Christian knights fought for the hand of Moorish ladies and Christian maids willingly gave themselves in marriage to Muslims. This religious camaraderie is remarkable, considering that during the same period adherents of both faiths in other lands were locked in mortal combat.

By the time the Spanish armies were poised on the borders of Granada, centuries of intermarriage and cultural diffusion had left their mark. While the Christians assimilated the philosophy, artistic influences, language, and many of the customs of the Moors (there are over 4,000 words of Arab origin in modern Spanish), the Granadinos had absorbed equally as many Spanish characteristics. Arabic was still the language of prestige and theology, but much of the populace spoke a vulgar Romance dialect. In spite of Koranic prohibition, the Moors also drank wine. As early as the 11th century, they were castigated by the Almoravid warrior Yusuf al-Tashufin for intemperance. The Granadinos had also adopted much of the dress and many of the manners of the Christian Spanish and biologically they were indistinct, save for the few Moors who were the offspring of Negro slaves. Religion alone was the truly deciding factor between both peoples.

For more than two centuries Granada had kept its independence by observing a wavering vassalage to the Castilian crown. The obeisance he was forced to render galled Sultan Muley Abul Hassan. Taking advantage of the discord which marked the end of the reign of Henry the Impotent, Isabel's strange half brother, the Sultan ceased the customary tribute. This act went un-

challenged in the initial years of the reign of Ferdinand
and Isabel, who were hard-pressed by a Portuguese
war of succession, but in 1478 they sent an emissary to
Granada to demand the arrears. Don Juan de Vera was
greeted at the Alhambra with a display of might and
Muley Abul growled, "Tell your sovereigns that the
Sultans of Granada, who used to pay tribute in money
to the Castilian crown, are dead. Our mint at present
coins nothing but blades of scimitars and heads of
lances."

The Moor's insolence outraged the monarchs but
their internal problems were far too weighty. They ignored the rebuff but the sagacious Ferdinand vowed,
"I shall pluck out the seeds of the pomegranate one by
one." And while Muley Abul Hassan contentedly sur-
veyed the prosperity of his domain and flexed his mus-
cles over the new strength he had found in the unchal-
lenged rebuttal, a bitter struggle which had been underway for years within his harem was about to explode.

In his youth Muley Abul Hassan had married his
cousin Aixa, a princess of the royal house. His interest
in the sultana waned after the birth of Boabdil, whom
his astrologers had doomed to misfortune, and his ardor
froze completely after the passing of Aixa's beauty. In
later years he took into his harem a Castilian noble-
woman named Fatima who had been captured in infancy and raised a Muslim. Her true name was Isabel.
In tribute to her bright blonde beauty, the Moors
called her Zoraya, Star of the Dawn. She bore Muley
Abul Hassan two sons, Cad and Nazar.

Ambitious and crafty, Zoraya eventually won ascend-
ancy over the Sultan and conspired to secure the
throne for her sons. As the first sultana, Aixa ruled the
harem with an iron fist and she and Zoraya, whom she
disdainfully called "*La Romiya*," the Christian, clashed
constantly. Tradition has it that Aixa was "*alta y*

King Ferdinand

morena, con ojos grandes y negros; cejijunta," tall dark, with large black eyes; eyebrows meeting. The last was a prerequisite in the Moorish ideal of beauty. Renowned for her virtue, Aixa was called *"La Horra,"* the Chaste, but virtue had nothing to do with the bloody manner in which she combated the vicious stratagems of her rival.

In their intrigues to secure the throne for their respective offsprings, both women sought out powerful allies. In Aixa's corner were the noble family of the Abencerrages and Aben Comixa, Commander of the Alhambra. Zoraya had the backing of Abul Cacem, the Grand Vizier, who was also of Christian descent, his brother General Reduan Vanegas, and the royal house of the Zegris.

With these factions locked in battle within the Alhambra, how often must the melancholy Boabdil have contemplated the inscription his ancestor had ordered engraved on the walls of the palace, "God alone is victor." As a boy, his father had treated him with paternal curiosity, but as he grew older Boabdil found himself relegated to the farthest corner of the throne-room. His mother was his comfort and protector, demanding the respect due her son as the crown prince. But even before the advent of his half brothers Boabdil was aware of his father's aversion and the sneering homage of the courtiers. His marriage to the delicate Moraima, daughter of Ali Atar, Alcayde of Loja, had been heralded more in that city than Granada.

By the time he had reached his 20th year, Boabdil had acquitted himself well enough in tournaments but he was more a sybarite than a warrior. He took up arms only for an occasional hunt in the Alpujarras. Often he sallied out to the *vega* with his younger brother, Aben Haxig, to play at falconry, but more than all else he loved the honeyed cadences of Arab verse or the mournful strains of the *oud* in the hands of a handsome troubadour.

Had he but a glimmer of foresight, Muley Abul Hassan would have paid serious attention to the dissension that was turning his palace into a battleground, but he set his sights beyond the borders of his realm. Pugnacious by nature, and spurred by the apparent weaknesses of his hereditary enemies, he decided to attack the strategic Castilian fortress of Zahara.

Ignoring the warnings of his advisors, Muley Abul Hassan burst out of Granada in October, 1481, and he stormed and plundered the fortress. He butchered the inhabitants and returned loaded with plunder, dragging behind him a host of slaves. Flaming with victory, he dispatched a message to the Barbary Powers calling for a *jihad* or holy war against the Infidels. Muley Abul Hassan could not have chosen a more inopportune time to open hostilities. Ferdinand and Isabel had settled their internal problems and were at that moment consolidating their forces. In a matter of weeks, a vast Spanish army was poised on the borders of Granada.

The Moors shuddered. Years of peace and prosperity had been shattered because the sultan had first defied the Castilians and then initiated an unnecessary conflagration. Instead of uniting the Granadinos, victory at Zahara had sown the seeds of civil war.

With the kingdom's security at stake this was hardly the time for internal conflict, but Aixa, perceiving the precariousness of the sultan's position, set her agents to work in sparking popular unrest, to oust her husband and bring Boabdil to the throne. The Alhambra itself was threatened with rebellion. Zoraya gave the alarm and the sultan, boiling with rage, had Aixa restricted to the harem and the hapless Boabdil imprisoned in the Tower of Comares. While the old man brooded, Zoraya intimated that Boabdil's execution would allay all of his internal problems.

Aixa anticipated her rival's strategy, however, and

gaining access to the tower she tied together her shawls and scarves and those of her attendants and lowered the perplexed prince down to the steep, rocky hillside below. Waiting Abencerrages spirited Boabdil away to Guadix.

The Christian legions, meanwhile, crossed the frontier and captured Alhama, a strategic town not far from Granada. Muley Abul Hassan set forth with an army of 50,000 to recapture the prize. The Muslims were felled by withering fire and were bitterly apprised of a reality which would mark the ensuing ten years of conflict; while they leaned to arrows and scimitars, the Christians were better armed and bolstered by powerful artillery. The sultan retreated to Granada with his defeated army and shut himself up in the Alhambra.

The walls of the harem had never been a barrier to Aixa and she had her agents busy scurrying through the city calling for her husband's overthrow. Soon pitched battles were being fought between the partisans of Boabdil and those of his father. Aixa rallied wavering nobles to her standard and when she was assured the way was clear she sent word to Boabdil; a civil war was raging in the capital and the people were ready to acclaim him as their rightful ruler.

Boabdil bore no great affection for his father but it is very likely he returned to Granada sincerely convinced that peace and order would return if he were to claim the throne. He entered the city in triumph. The royal guards were driven from the Alhambra and Muley Abul Hassan was forced to retreat to Malaga where he was joined by his younger brother "El Zagal," the Valiant, as well as powerful nobles and allies of Zoraya.

The Alhambra's tinkling fountains never sounded sweeter to Aixa. Normally, executions would be the order of the day but Boabdil forbade bloodshed. The haughty sultana had to content herself with watching her enemies grovel in homage to her son, vowing their allegiance, which, she warned the gullible Boabdil, "was as empty as their hearts."

While the Moors were occupied with internal dissension, the Spanish sovereigns laid siege to Loja and ravaged the surrounding *vega*. They stationed an armada in the Straits of Gibraltar with orders to sweep from the sea all Moorish vessels. With the Christians over the frontier, aid cut off from North Africa, and his father and uncle plotting to regain the throne, Boabdil's hold was tenuous, to say the least, but his star was rising. His father-in-law Ali Atar, in command of Loja, was a fiery veteran of countless battles. He inflicted a major defeat on the Spaniards and forced them to withdraw across the border. Since he had pledged his allegiance to his son-in-law, the victory belonged to Sultan Boabdil.

Hoping to win back his popularity, Muley Abul Hassan ravaged the Andalusian fiefs of the Duke of Medina Sidonia and he defeated a vainglorious Christian regiment which had attacked Malaga. It wasn't long before the fickle Granadinos were mumbling that the old sultan was a true defender of the Faith while Boabdil preferred the perfumed baths of the Alhambra to the field of battle. Aixa convinced her son that in order to retain the throne he would have to outdo his father's exploits and carry the war into Christian Spain. Boabdil would have preferred a truce with the Castilians but Aixa would have none of it. She had mastered one Isabel; she would vanquish another.

Following his mother's advice, Boabdil assembled a large army and took the field in ostentatious splendor. He was mounted on a magnificent Arabian steed and his armor sparkled in the sun. With a scimitar of Damascus steel securely at his side, he also carried a ponderous, if impressive, lance. But for all the pomp, Boabdil's inexperienec was evident. As he passed through the Gate of Elvira, his lance broke against the

*Boabdil surrendering Granada
to Ferdinand and Isabella*

arch. This was viewed as an evil omen and his officers entreated him to turn back. No doubt feeling his mother's sharp black eyes riveted on his back, Boabdil scoffed at their superstition. He drew his scimitar and led the way "in an arrogant and haughty style."

At Loja, Boabdil's army was reinforced by Ali Atar's veterans and the novice welcomed the advice of the old warhorse. Lucena was chosen as the target of attack, and as the Moors drew up outside the city they were met by a Christian force under the Count of Cabra. A mist obscured the Spaniards and when Boabdil questioned Ali Atar as to the identity of the enemy banners, the old man mistook the standard of the Count of Cabra (a goat) for that of Baeza and Ubeda (a dog), concluding that the armies of both these large cities had joined the defenders and consequently "all Castile" was upon them. In the ensuing confusion, the Moors were beaten into retreat, Boabdil strove to rally his troops but the Spaniards continued to surge forward. Ali Atar fell on the banks of the Genil, slashing away, and Boabdil surrendered.

The news of his son's inglorious defeat was scarcely out of the mouth of the courier when Muley Abul Hassan set out for Granada. Aixa, accepting the inevitable, claimed royal immunity and set up residence in the *alcazar* of the Albaicin, the city's poorest quarter but the one most loyal to her son.

While captive in Lucena, Boabdil received gracious notes from the Spanish sovereigns who fully perceived the value of their hostage. In a burst of gratitude, *"El Rey Chico"* is reputed to have told a messenger, "Tell my sovereigns, the king and queen, that I cannot be unhappy being in the power of such high and mighty princes, especially since they partake so largely of that grace and goodness which Allah bestows upon the monarchs whom he greatly loves. Tell them further, that I had long thought of submitting myself to their sway, to receive the Kingdom of Granada from their hands . . ."

Such music must have indeed sounded sweet but the monarchs were composing another tune for their captive to play. Boabdil would be far more useful free as a rival for the throne than a pampered prisoner. The sovereigns bided their time, and as soon as the Sultana Aixa offered ransom they set in motion their master plan. To test Boabdil's power, they launched an army across the frontier with orders to lay waste the land. The *vega* of Granada was ravaged to the gates of the city. Fearful that Aixa and her allies would take possession of the Alhambra in his absence, Muley Abul Hassan dared not challenge the Christians. He watched the destruction from his "Crimson Fortress," gnashing his teeth in frustration.

Convinced that Boabdil's influence was indeed potent, the Spanish sovereigns accepted Aixa's proposal and Ferdinand drew up a treaty which was a masterpiece of diplomatic expertise. Boabdil was to become a vassal of the Castilian crown, deliver up 14,000 ducats of gold and 7,000 Christian captives, and turn his son over as hostage; in return, he would be recognized the ruler of all those Moorish cities which would acknowledge him and he could call upon the Castilians for aid. But here was the most adroit stroke: the treaty would not take effect until Boabdil repossessed the capital.

"*El Rey Chico*" was regally outfitted and conducted to the border. Aixa's agents met him and he was secreted into the Albaicin. She roused the Abencerrages and called for an uprising against Muley Abul Hassan. The entire city was ablaze. The carnage reached such a peak that the *Alfaquis,* doctors of the Faith, called for a truce, warning that further bloodshed would split the kingdom assunder and leave it at the mercy of the Spaniards. They entreated Boabdil to retire to Almeria, leaving his father in control of the capital. Aixa denounced this compromise but Boabdil had no recourse. The skill of Ferdinands' tactic was obvious. The Spanish monarch had plucked the first seeds of the pomegranate.

In an effort to win popular support once and for all, Muley Abul Hassan called for a *jihad* into Christian Andalusia. A powerful force was assembled in Ronda, bolstered by savage Mauretanian Berbers. The invasion was repulsed and Ferdinand's retaliation was immediate. The Spanish re-captured Zahara and foraged into the fertile uplands, leaving a desert in their wake. Alora and Sentenil fell and Muley Abul Hassan was overawed by news of the pillage and destruction as thousands of refugees poured into the capital. Returning in triumph to Cordova, the wily Ferdinand ordered his generals to assist Boabdil in every way possible to wrest the throne from his father.

For a time Boabdil enjoyed a feeble, contented court in Almeria but news that his father was felled by a paralytic stroke shocked him out of inertia. *"El Zagal"* had taken command of the armies and with the throne within his grasp he decided to eliminate his hated nephew. He stormed into Almeria. Finding that Boabdil had escaped to Cordova, he slew Prince Aben Haxig and Aixa was borne back as a prisoner to the capital.

These royal contentions were becoming irksome to the Spanish monarchs and they decided to accelerate the pace of the war. They brought in gunsmiths from France, Germany, and Italy to reinforce their artillery, and in the spring of 1485 they launched a vicious attack against Ronda. After ten days of nightmare siege the city surrendered. But this Christian victory only stiffened the resolution of the Moors who then rallied to *"El Zagal."*

Informed of this new dissension, Ferdinand suddenly developed a tender interest in Boabdil. He suggested that *"El Rey Chico"* return to Granada with the aid of

Castilian arms and gold. With his father dead and his uncle his avowed enemy, Boabdil now had a genuine sense of righteousness in claiming the throne. Most of all, like all Moors he had inherited the aggressive individualism of the desert Bedouin, and Ferdinand strummed on this defect like a musician. Boabdil took the bait and, as Ferdinand anticipated, his presence in the kingdom breathed fire on the internal friction. As the new conflagration mounted in intensity, news arrived that the Spanish armies were gathering for another invasion and the *Alfaquis* prevailed upon both factions to cease hostilities.

The Castilians turned their concentration to the east where "*El Zagal*" was entrenched. They met vehement resistance at Baza. Worse, they were plagued by the harsh Andalusian winter, with its flash floods and freak storms. By all logic they should have lost the campaign, but a miracle happened, one that may well have been brought about through greasing of Moorish palms. Baza capitulated. More, "*El Zagal*" surrendered Guadix and Almeria. In return, he was to be named King of Andarax, retain his wealth, and govern a tiny kingdom in the Alpujarras with 2,000 *Mudejar* subjects.

"*El Zagal's*" surrender and the fall of Malaga confused already shaky loyalties and panic gripped the Moorish capital. The Moors knew that emotionally Granada was the focus of Spanish ambitions. Ferdinand wrote Boabdil, and "*El Rey Chico*" appraised the Spanish king of the explosive situation and requested that he be allowed to retain the crown. Blasting Boabdil as faithless, Ferdinand called for the immediate surrender of the city; to show his contempt he addressed the demand to the generals and *Alfaquis*. The Moors replied that they preferred death rather than surrender the pearl of Islam.

After devastating the surrounding *vega* and cutting off all supply routes to the city, a vast Spanish army encamped before the doomed jewel of Granada in the spring of 1491. In a last thrust of hate, *"El Zagal"* joined the Christians. But the Granadinos would not succumb so lightly. Individualism to the side, they rallied to Boabdil. Fired by their enthusiasm, *"El Rey Chico"* actually sallied forth and razed the Christian fortress at Alhendin, following this with the capture of two more towns. At no time had he acted with a greater sense of purpose. Even Aixa was dumbfounded.

But there was a tenderness in Boabdil which, while laudable, defeated his political awareness. He had given asylum to Zoraya and his half brothers after his father's death; now he was moved by an emotion which would prove his undoing. Fatima, the beautiful niece of Aben Comixa, had been captured by the Count of Tendilla. The vizier begged the sultan to help him free her and Boabdil, without hesitation, paid the huge ransom. The count had treated the doe-eyed captive royally and, in gratitude, the Moorish vizier wrote him, thereby initiating an amicable and eventually traitorous correspondence.

Despite Boabdil's modest military successes, the capital was still surrounded. Convinced that his North African compatriots would come to Granada's aid if a port were freed for their entry, Boabdil beat a march through the Christian lines and bore down on Salobrena. The *Mudejares* threw open the gates and the Spanish garrison retreated to the Alcazar. Learning that Ferdinand's army was in full march to relieve the defenders, Boabdil was forced to return to Granada, but his audacity rekindled Moorish hostility and the Spanish were forced to put down uprisings in Baza, Guadix, and Almeria. Even *"El Zagal's"* subjects rose up and drove the traitor out of his domain. With the permission of their Catholic Majesties, he packed up his treasures and headed for Morocco where the Caliph of Fez had him blinded and thrown into the streets.

With the coming of winter, the Spaniards prepared for a long siege. They hesitated to direct their artillery on the lovely jewel and they were aware that a direct attack would be costly and perhaps fatal. They decided to starve out the inhabitants. The blockade was tightened and the thinnest vine was uprooted lest it give subsistence to the Moors. With the smell of death in the air, the Muslims grew more daring. They challenged Christian knights to personal combat. Since they were vicious hand-to-hand opponents they frequently emerged victorious.

There were displays of valor on both sides. A Moor charged into the Christian camp and flung a lance inches from the royal tent; it carried a note that it had been intended for the Queen. To avenge Isabel, Christian knights stole into Granada and drove a dagger into the door of the great mosque with a note pinned to it reading *Ave Maria*. The months dragged on and one hot summer day a cheer went up from the city's battlements. The tent camp of the Spaniards had caught fire and in moments was a silken holocaust. But Muslim joy was brief. To show their resolution, Ferdinand and Isabel built a city of stone on the very spot. It was laid out in the form of a cross and christened Santa Fe, Holy Faith.

Boabdil was now sitting on a powder keg. The city was beginning to feel the pangs of famine. Aben Comixa, induced by the Count of Tendilla, urged the sultan to surrender. Aixa demanded that he fight on. Boabdil retained a faint hope that help would arrive from Egypt or Morocco, but the nobles were growing impatient. There were also signs of pestilence and hysteria was mounting. Boabdil decided to negotiate.

A treaty was signed on November 25, 1491, in which he agreed to surrender the city in 60 days. The terms were lenient. The Granadinos would be allowed to practice their religion and live in peace as *Mudejares*, or leave, as thousands had done in the past, for Africa. Boabdil was accorded the dukedom of Guadix; he would retain his personal possessions and receive 30,0000 *castellanos* of gold. Equal terms were afforded the Sultana Aixa and Zoraya. Later Isabel convinced Zoraya to return to Christianity and her sons became Spanish nobles.

As the desperate Granadinos wrested with their fate, Boabdil appeared before the great mosque and in a voice wracked with sorrow said, "It was my crime in ascending the throne in rebellion against my father, which has brought these woes upon the kingdom; but Allah has grieviously visited my sins upon my head. For your sake, my people, I have made this treaty, to protect you from the sword, your little ones from famine, your wives and daughters from outrage; and to secure you the enjoyment of your properties . . . and your religion. . . ."

Fearful that further delay would mean calamity, Boabdil asked that the formal surrender take place on January 2 instead of on January 6, but to the end Aixa was adamant. She sent word to the Spanish that her son would never stoop to the humiliation of kissing the hand of the Infidel king and unless this part of the customary ceremony was modified, means would be found to resist the surrender. Ferdinand and Isabel conceded.

As the rising sun appeared over the snowy Sierra Nevada, signal guns boomed from the Alhambra, signifying the surrender of the lovely jewel. At the approach of the Spanish army, with Ferdinand and Isabel at its head, followed by the Grand Cardinal of Spain, Boabdil rode forth. The end had come. *"El Rey Chico"* had one last request: that the portal from which he left his beloved Alhambra be closed forever.

Boabdil's fate, however, was not sealed with Aixa's legendary recrimination. He took up residence in the Valley of Purchena and appeared quite content. Loyal cavaliers joined him as well as his "faithful" Vizier Aben Comixa. The delicate Moraima sorrowed away from *pesadumbre* but Aixa remained steadfast at the side of her son. As news came to them that the Catholic sovereigns had reneged on the treaty and were imposing the Inquisition, Aixa was full of foreboding. Soon the fearful proclamation echoed throughout Granada: accept baptism or face expulsion.

The Jews, who had been the traditional allies of the Moors, were the first to go. Thousands of *Mudejares* renounced Islam while thousands more fled to Africa. The Inquisition cast its shadow on Boabdil's tiny realm. It no longer pleased their Catholic Majesties to allow such potential danger to go unheeded. They had no illusions that many of their Moorish subjects were false converts. Boabdil was a dangerous example. It was suggested that he become a *Converso*, but he refused.

Ferdinand decided on another tactic. Aben Comixa had been pawned off by the Count of Tendilla on Hernando de Zafra, the king's secretary, and they daily exchanged letters detailing Boabdil's movements. Ferdinand arranged a scandalous pact with Aben Comixa on March 17, 1493. As Boabdil's agent, and without his knowledge, the vizier signed away his lord's estates for 80,000 gold ducats and agreed that the entire Moorish royal household depart for Africa.

The betrayal overwhelmed Boabdil. Heartsick, he set sail for Morocco where he was welcomed by his kinsman, the Caliph of Fez, who had dealt such terrible retribution to *"El Zagal."* Weary of intrigue, Aixa went into seclusion. Boabdil is said to have lived 34 years in Fez where he built an Alcazar to emulate the fragile beauties of the Alhambra. Spain's last Moorish ruler died in battle in the year 1536, leading the armies of his kinsman on the banks of the Guad-al-Hawit, "dying in defense of the kingdom of another, after wanting in spirit to die in defense of his own."

The Irish rebel, Tyrone of Ulster

TYRONE
OF ULSTER

By Angela Stuart

*S*hortly after Elizabeth came
to the throne in 1558, she may have caught glimpses of
a small Gaelic boy as he "trooped the streets of London
with a goodly equipage." His name was Hugh O'Neill
and he had a lineage quite as royal as that of Elizabeth, being heir presumptive to the kingship of Ulster
which had been with the O'Neill family since 1201.
The north of Ireland where the O'Neills held sway was
the only section of the island which had successfully resisted English invasion and settlement. The royal forces
had never penetrated this fastness of dense woods and
quaking bogs. Here the old Gaelic world, speaking its
own language and preserving its own culture, made a
last stand. Ulster lords were pure, "mere Irishe" in the
Elizabethan phrase. Henry VIII, casting a covetous
glance at the unsubdued north, conferred the Earldom

61

of Tyrone upon Hugh O'Neill's grandfather, Conn O'Neill, in the hope of annexing Ulster to the crown, but nothing came of it.

Rivalry within families was fierce in Ireland, especially in the intensely Celtic north. By the time Hugh O'Neill was nine both his father and elder brother had been murdered in a clan feud over the succession. At this point the English government in Dublin decided upon a bold experiment. Sir Henry Sydney had just completed his term as the queen's lord deputy in Ireland. Before sailing home, he lifted the fledgling chieftain, Hugh O'Neill, out of Dungannon Castle in the wilds of Ulster and carried him back to London, there to be "fostered by the heat of Her Majesty's favour unto nobility and counselors with other great men and captains." At this time Sydney spoke of his ward as "just a little boy, very poor of goods and full feebly friended."

But Hugh had a precocious mind and set himself to absorbing all the civility he could in the great houses where he lived in London and the country—Sydney's Penhurst and the earl of Leicester's Kenilworth. For eight formative years he was exposed to the new comfort, lavishness, delicacy, and refinement of the then modern Tudor society. In March of 1567, when he was 17, a youth of middle height with blazing red hair and the fine physique of the Gael, he sailed back to Ireland.

In spring the undulating bog-land of Ulster was shiny black underfoot with swathes of rich yellow and mauve-blue gorse. Gulls from the lakes followed the churls' ploughs and there was a smell of peat on every breeze. The ancestral hold of the north upon O'Neill was the strongest factor in his makeup, and would never be relinquished. But the contrasts with Elizabethan England he met at every turn were overwhelming. He had been exposed to the Renaissance with learning and the arts bursting into the greatest flower-

Robert Devereux, Earl of Essex

ing of all the seasons they were ever to know. And he had come home to the Dark Ages.

Officially, he was baron of Dungannon, the O'Neill family seat, with a maintenance of 1000 marks a year from the crown, but Dungannon was by no means a castle in the English sense. The walls were of clay and frequently exposed their tree-bough anatomies. A fire in the center of the great hall smoked vaguely up to the central vent in the roof. Rooms were lighted, if at all, by malodorous candles made of butter and reeds. Beds were heaps of straw. Cooking, never a Celtic art, was barbaric.

At London tables O'Neill had enjoyed dishes seasoned with all the spices of the East, as well as rare fruits—quinces from Orleans, apricots from Armenia, plums from Syria, cherries from Damascus. In Dungannon the staple diet was Irish stew made with all the entrails in the pot swimming about with great greasy lumps of butter. Even the milk was strained through unclean straw. There was a pastoral touch in summer when food was served out-of-doors on beaten fern tables—castigated by the English as mounds of wet grass.

At the time of O'Neill's return to Ulster, the English had been trying to consolidate their rule in Ireland for four centuries. Ironically, the first English to arrive in Ireland came by invitation. In 1167, King Dermot of Leinster engaged a band of Anglo-Normans from south Wales to aid him in his war against a rival chieftain. Norman swords promptly won a decisive victory for Dermot, and in gratitude he gave these foreign allies rich fiefs. But this only whetted their appetites.

The Normans had a genius for conquest and Ireland was a tempting prize. Not only was it far more fertile than Scotland, but the limestone plain which made up half its soil formed the best grazing land in Europe. As more Anglo-Norman bands crossed St. George's channel, the invaders extended their spearhead until by 1207 Norman-conquered lands covered half the island. Everything south and east of a line drawn from Limerick to Lough Neagh and Coleraine was English territory.

But then the mercurial Celts fought back savagely. Within a hundred years after the Norman conquest of 1170, Gaelic chiefs had recovered large parts of their former lordships in hundreds of petty battles. Ireland, the English learned, was easy to overrun, but a difficult country to hold.

Upon the accession of Henry VIII in 1509, anarchic Ireland lay wide open to reconquest. English power had been contracted to a strip some 20 miles to the west and north of Dublin, known as the Pale. It was the richest, most settled and civilized part of the country—the only place where English was spoken or even understood. The inhabitants of the strip were known as "gentlemen of the Pale and loyal Irish." The heart of the oasis was Dublin Castle, the stronghold of English government in Ireland without a break from 1170 until December 6, 1922, when the Union Jack was lowered from above the castle (it was the first time the English ensign came down in 150 years) and the Irish Free State flag was hoisted in its stead.

Beyond the Pale the king's writ hardly ran. Most of the neighboring Anglo-Norman knights lived "Irishly," having become so intermingled with the aboriginal Celts they had lost all traces of their Norman origin. The crown depended upon the powerful Anglo-Norman earls of Ormond, Kildare, and Desmond for cooperation in parts beyond the Pale. But their help was fitful, disingenuous, and never hearty. They were inclined to be earls or clan chiefs as suited them best. An English captain complained, "In short, in this kingdom there is neither justice nor right and everyone does what he pleases."

To Henry VIII his Irish realm was far from profitable, being "full of the King's decayed rents and embezzled lands." Still, he renounced the idea of a fresh conquest, adopting instead a policy known as "Surrender and Re-Grant." Irish chiefs were induced to surrender the independent tenure of their lands and then receive them back as grantees of the crown, along with a title of the king's earl, baron, or knight. But Henry gained little by their allegiance. No mere patent of English nobility could restrain the fury of Irish broils. As Edmund Spenser, the English poet living in Ireland, wrote of these outbursts between clan and clan: "Whensoever they make head, no laws, no penalties can restrain, but what they do in the violence of that fury tread down and trample underfoot all, both divine and human things."

In the English Reformation Parliament of 1529-1536, Henry made the great breach with Rome and proceeded to set up a church "Catholic without the Pope" throughout his realm. When it became apparent to Rome that Henry was not going to return to the fold, Jesuits visited Ireland for the first time in 1541, and the idea was born that Ireland must be kept true to the faith, whatever the cost might be. To the tribulations of reimposing English royal authority in the westernmost isle, was added from Henry VIII's Reformation onwards, the fateful divisions of religious beliefs.

Reared in England and backed by English money, the young Hugh O'Neill settled down to try to make the best of two worlds—Renaissance and Medieval. Suave memories of the years in London had left their indelible mark. But before long he would discover he had set himself an insuperable task. The antipathy between the two cultures, Gaelic and Elizabethan, was too elemental to be bridged since there was scarcely a point of contact between their traditions, their ideals, their art, their jurisprudence, or their social life.

O'Neill went down to Dublin regularly to attend Parliament and maintained important friendships with English nobles outside his local sphere. He was said to have "a great party in the English Pale" due to the mesmerism of his personal charm. In 1570, when the everlasting squabbles over land between the great Anglo-Norman nobles in the south flamed into rebellion, he was painfully caught in a dual loyalty. Nevertheless, he led a troop of horse in the queen's pay against his fellow Irishmen. To the government the southern uprisings were the madness of mad dogs. O'Neill's seeming complacency while the royal forces burned, hung, and slew where and when they could was only a mask. He knew he was not strong enough by himself to face English solidarity, so for the time being he held aloof.

The fact remained that all O'Neill had witnessed in London of the lustful ambitions of the great nobles, the opportunism of even a Puritan like Sydney, and the utter ruthlessness of a Raleigh had gone so far toward shaping his character that he could never lapse back into the mold of his ancestors. He could not content himself with a life of spoliation and cattle-raiding. In rearing O'Neill for a tool of imperial expansion the English had overreached the mark.

With his subtle, calculating mind he would formulate his plans in the secrecy of his Ulster stronghold, consolidating his power with a patience and cunning that made him a match for Elizabeth herself. Irish unity was the all-in-all behind his plotting and his long machinations with Rome, with Spain, with the Scottish Highlands. His great aim was to break through tribalism and establish an Irish confederation—to forge the welter of clans with their maze of alliances and entanglements into a sovereign kingdom. That he came within a hair's breadth of his goal is the climax of 16th-century Ireland.

O'Neill early gained a reputation among the English of the Pale as an arch-dissembler. Although for 16 years he made dutiful submission to the queen, there were officals in the government who did not quite trust him. Elizabeth, who no doubt saw too many of her own traits reflected in this labyrinthine Celt, disliked him from the start. Still, O'Neill forwarded his own case so well with the English that at 35 he was made earl of Tyrone by the Parliament in Dublin. With the earldom he acquired an immense territory, its vassalage, its rents, and its political influence so that by a single stroke, O'Neill, who would be known from then on as Tyrone, became an Irish feudal baron of the greatest power.

The Councillors in the Pale looked at the map of Ulster with some uneasiness. It was the most unalleviatedly Celtic part of the country, the stronghold of the clans. A world unto itself, it had been cut off from the rest of Ireland from prehistoric times behind its barriers of lakes, bogs, rivers, and dense forests, all impassable except by those born and bred to their uncharted ways. In the 16th century there were no towns, few buildings, and no roads—only muddy, beaten paths. Most of the rude inhabitants had never seen an Englishman.

Royal troops could go almost anywhere in the south without hindrance, but Ulster was what the English called "fast"—that is, secure against them by its natural wildness and its nearness to the Hebridean Scots. To guard themselves, the government insisted that a fort be built on the Blackwater River, the largest natural barrier that any force entering the heart of Tyrone's country had to cross. However, they relied less upon an isolated garrison than upon the earl's rival kinsmen, and all the internecine feuds in the north, to hold him in check. It was the balance of power which Elizabeth and her statesmen understood so coldly.

There was another matter highly disturbing to the

English—the title "The O'Neill" to which Tyrone had succeeded as clan chieftain. The O'Neill was the most famous of all Irish names, entailing not only clan loyalty, but military service and tributes by which in time of war the O'Neill could bring out the whole armed forces of his freemen and commandeer food supplies. While the government pressed him to abjure the title because of its conflicting pretensions with his patent of nobility, he never complied. So to the English he was the earl of Tyrone, and to the Irish the O'Neill.

Elizabeth's Irish wars began some ten years after her accession and only ended as she lay on her deathbed. For her Ireland was always "that running sore of rebellion." She hated the vast expenditure of treasure needed for the re-conquest. English troops "raw and of the last levy" were always arriving in Dublin. But as fast as armies were created, they decayed and vanished. Ireland swallowed them up as if they had sunk in her bogs. To finance the Irish campaigns the queen had taken out foreign loans at biting interest, sold lands left and right—those which had come to the crown from Henry's dissolution of the monasteries, royal duchies, and even her personal jewels. Little as she had to show for it, politics forced her to continue the struggle.

The pope was Elizabeth's declared enemy since in the eyes of Rome she was illegitimate—the child of an invalid marriage and therefore not a lawful queen. Rome, as a world power acting chiefly through Spain, was set upon breaking England, the chief champion of Protestantism. And so long as Ireland was unconquered, it was always a suitable base for a Catholic invasion of England. The Spaniards were capable of carrying all the way from their home ports to Irish harbors an army big enough to swing the balance in Ireland against the power of the English crown. Individual Spanish ships bringing arms and munitions to a rebel leader might lie for days in some of the western inlets of the sea before a report reached Dublin. Ireland, as Sir Walter Raleigh said, was "the defence next the heart" —the weak spot in England's armament.

Elizabethan conquest and colonization went hand-in-hand as the crown deprived natives of their lands and drove them from their homes to make room for English settlers. But the plantations proved abortive. It was the way of the Irish to creep back to their own lands after the English colonists had been raided and patiently begin tilling the soil again.

Cattle were the country's gold, the chief Irish currency. The whole turbulent life of the countryside—raids and counter-raids, the ambitions of clan chieftains, great battles—all centered about these lowing mobs of cows. The churls, or peasants, lived in earthern huts with thatched roofs (swine-sties, the English called them). They slept upon the ground on rushes newly cut and full of water and lice. According to a ship-wrecked captain of a Spanish armada, "They do not eat oftener than once a day and this is at night; and that which they usually eat is butter with oaten bread. They drink sour-milk, for they have no other drink; they don't drink water although it is the best in the world. On feast days they eat some flesh half-cooked without bread or salt."

Still, all visitors agreed the Irish were a comely looking people. The men, "tall as Roman spears and swift as deer," wore a kilt and shirt of saffron color with a long, shaggy cloak buckled at the shoulder. The Irish custom of wearing *glibbs*—a thick mass of hair over their eyes—made disguise easy, detection difficult. When interrogated they would pull forward their *glibbs* so their eyes should not betray them if they lied. Hence the constant English legislation against the wearing of *glibbs* and long Irish mantles (in which weapons were easily concealed) and the efforts to enforce English dress. Everywhere the English colonists

Queen Elizabeth I

saw room for improvement, but the Irish preferred to keep things as they were and occupied themselves in preying upon the improvers.

As the 16th century waned, the eyes of Dublin Castle were turned more and more inquiringly upon the earl of Tyrone. While the queen continued her aimless wars in the south and the Irish put their reliance in "castles of bones, not of stones," the earl apparently watched, waited, and did nothing. But behind his facade of loyalty to the government, he showed tireless ingenuity in building up his independent forces. He was so secretive Dublin was hardly aware how year after year he fought for land in order to create scores of liegemen. He even took for clients men who were nobles themselves. He was allowed to keep a garrison of 600 men in the queen's pay, but he changed them constantly so that an excessive number was trained and disciplined. Once he ordered a great quantity of lead to roof his castle and then turned it into bullets.

Whenever he went hunting or fowling his company carried extra guns. Along the way he stopped and chatted with any people he met. Finding they knew no weapons but spears, bows and arrows, he would produce a gun, explain its use, and bid them try if they could manage it. He would praise anyone who was handy, give him a piece of money, and sometimes even the weapon itself. The people were so delighted they would practice assiduously, scraping up bullets and gunpowder where they could. It was the nucleus of a rough army that grew with the years.

Tyrone's dissembling was on the whole successful, except in the matter of religion. He was as Gaelic by descent as a man could be, and like every Irish Gael, he was a Catholic—which was reason enough for Elizabeth and her counselors to regard him as a probable enemy. Spies reported to Dublin that he was fostering the Counter Reformation by communication with the

Continent and Philip II. There were even rumors of secret importations from Spain into the western creeks of ducats, powder, and men.

Tyrone was enraged by these informers whom the government dispatched to Ulster to pry into his private affairs. When his clansmen caught an English spy of some note, the earl stood by and watched while they hung him from a thorn tree. For an Irishman, even though he was a noble, to hang an English subject was rash in the extreme. Tyrone was immediately summoned to London to give an accounting of the execution and other matters disturbing to the government. The queen would not look at him, but he appeared before the Privy Council.

He answered their endless questions and probings with his "high, dissembling, subtle and profound wit." He could be irresistible when he chose, and in the end they simply sent him back to Ireland with orders to behave himself. Specifically he was told he must try to bring his people to adopt English habits, wear English dress, and cut the obnoxious *glibb* through which they looked as through a visor. He must stop communicating with the Scots, and he must allow his land to be shired like any English county—all of which he postponed putting into practice.

Incidents kept cropping up that brought collisions with the government. When Spanish ships fleeing an English naval battle were driven onto the Irish coast in autumn of 1586, an order went out from the Pale that no quarter be given any Spaniard who escaped the wrecks. The natives, gripped by hysteria, fell on the strangers as they came clambering by the hundreds out of the sea, battered them down on the rocks, spilling their blood into sandy shorewaters.

Such inhumanity was too much for Tyrone. Standing on his right as an independent nobleman, he went with a great herd of cattle to feed the castaways who had survived at Inishowen. Gathering up all he could, he got more than 2000 Spaniards safely away to Scotland. A month after the wrecks, a report from the Lord Deputy in the Pale to the Privy Council in London spoke for the first time of "a special distrust of the Earl of Tyrone."

The rescue of the Spanish castaways was risky enough, but Tyrone made a second and worse blunder as far as Dublin was concerned when he eloped with a young English girl, Mabel Bagenal, in the summer of 1591. The Bagenals were the earl's neighbors, if he could be said to have had any. They lived at the Newry, a former abbey which marked the practical boundary of settler penetration into Ulster—about five miles inland. Since Mabel's father, Sir Nicholas Bagenal, had been Tyrone's bitterest enemy, and her brother, Sir Henry Bagenal, the queen's marshal, continued the feud, it was an unfortunate household in which to choose a bride. Tyrone was twice the English girl's age and had already had two wives; but his rank was awesome, he was a striking figure in glinting mail on horseback, and like so many other women she succumbed to his lure. When Henry Bagenal forbade the marriage, Tyrone and a company of gentlemen abducted the bride.

But the marriage was too incongruous in race, rank, and religion to last. Mabel, a straitlaced puritan, was aghast at Gaelic ways—especially the custom of having highborn mistresses in the same household with the wife. She fled Dungannon and took refuge with her brother. Utterly broken by her experience, she died soon after. The earl was at a loss to understand her actions, merely, as he said, "because I affected two other gentlewomen." The tragic countess of Tyrone has been called "the Helen of the Elizabethan wars," and while she did not actually cause a war, she was one of the contributing causes to its outbreak. Henry Bagenal maintained his sister had been seduced and swore vengeance against the earl.

By winter of 1594, the rift between Tyrone and the government was unmistakable. He had an excellent secret service and received news from abroad before the lord deputy. When he learned the English were sending 2000 of their best veterans from Brittany for service in Ireland, he knew the Pale was making ready to invade Ulster. So he struck first, and in February, 1595, sent a force to demolish the English fort on the Blackwater, always "a great eyesore to him, lying on the chief passageway into his country." The clans, who had been champing at the bit, burst out at once, and the greatest of Elizabeth's Irish wars, which would be prolonged for eight years, was on.

Tyrone had drawn his sword slowly, with many a sidelong, backward glance. The lesser chieftains were driven by their intractable natures to fight the English, but each one fought a hopeless, isolated fight. With Tyrone it was different. He was wholly Celtic, but at the same time he had English breeding and came closer than any other Irishman in history to the cold rationalism of the Renaissance. He was furious at having to fight an English war, having an intelligent grasp of all that was at stake in such a conflict. But once he was in it, he fought like fury.

His Gaelic followers felt the edge of his temper as he took them by the scruff of the neck and transformed them from a mob of raiders into a drilled and disciplined army. He was the first Irish leader to bring into the field a force equipped after the best fashion of the times—and wearing red coats. It was written of him in the Pale: "His rebellion will be more dangerous and cost the queen more crowns than any that have foregone him since her reign began, for, educated in our discipline and naturally valiant, he is worthily reputed the best man of war of his nation. Most of his followers

are well-trained soldiers and he is the greatest man of
territory in the kingdom and absolute commander of
the north of Ireland."

Tyrone had three classes of fighting men: the cavalry, the *kernes* or light infantry, and Scotch *gallowglasses* or mercenaries who served as heavy infantry.
The cavalry were made up of the lord's kinsmen and
the gentlemen of the country. They wore only light mail
and rode without stirrups, but could not face English
horse except at the most favorable odds since the shock
of encounter would unhorse them. The native *kernes*
were unarmored and were trained for the first time as
musketeers. In a standup fight the *kerne* was normally
useless, but in the great bogs he hopped like a goat
from one firm tussock to another, while the Englishmen
simply drowned.

The Scotch *gallowglasses*, with their liberal admix-
ture of Norse blood, were the mainstay of the Irish
forces, feared and respected by the English who held it
easier to vanquish 600 Irish than 300 Scots. In Tyrone's
army the *gallowglasses* were brought up-to-date and
became pikemen. There was a constant coming and
going of Scots across the narrow waters dividing the
two countries. If hard-pressed in battle, the Scots
would summon reinforcements from the isles by lighting fires on the Irish cliffs.

During 1595-96 the war dragged on through parley
after parley on showery hillsides. Tyrone would patch
up a truce, prolong it, lure the Scots, fish for aid from
Spain. Then, in the summer of 1598, all the campaigns
reached a climax in the Battle of the Yellow Ford.
Again the objective was the Ulster bone of contention,
the fort on the Blackwater River. In August Tyrone
surrounded and completely blockaded the English garrison. The men were reduced to eating the greens that
grew on the sides of their sconce when Sir Henry Bagenal, spoiling to meet Tyrone and avenge his sister,

started northward with six regiments to lift the siege.

It was slow going since every road and river leading to the fort had been spiked or trenched by Tyrone. The woods were plashed and counter-plashed—woven together branch on branch. The English army, a long, straggling cavalcade of footmen and horses, with colors, ordinances, and *vivandieres,* came within sight of the fort. Men on the ramparts cheered and threw their hats in the air, expecting a square meal. Since the English had no choice of a road, they had to cross a little river at a place where the water ran discolored, known as the Yellow Ford. It was here they found themselves hotly engaged by the Irish.

Tyrone's force was covered by a bog, across which his musketeers passed with their usual agility. The two leading English regiments, although galled continually by the fire of the Irish on both their flanks, pushed on across the ford until they reached an open boggy space. But here Tyrone had dug an elaborate trench, a mile long, five feet deep, four feet wide, and surmounted by a thorn hedge. Regiment number one, raked from the trench, spread out, charged, and crossed. Beyond was a slope surmounted by a sconce, and down this slope came the onrush of Tyrone's horse to break the line that had already been frayed in taking the trench. The trench seemed to act as a guillotine, so that while regiment number one was being broken beyond it by the Irish horse, regiment number two was restrained by the Irish foot who had poured back to meet it. Bagenal lifted his visor to see more of what was happening. In that second a bullet caught him in the forehead and he was killed on the spot.

By this time the whole column was under attack. Back along the extended line—Bagenal had blundered in leaving an excessive space of 150 paces between the regiments—the center was in difficulty where a saker, the biggest cannon the English had, was stuck fast in

77

the bog. While oxen strained and tugged, Irish pikemen rushed in and hamstrung the poor beasts so that
the English never did get their gun loose. In the middle of the melee, a soldier in the main body went up to
the powder-cart to replenish his supply. A spark from
his torch dropped into the open barrel. A big explosion
followed, causing such confusion Bagenal's Irish com-
panies and some of the raw English reinforcements
began to run away, the Irish going straight over to
their countrymen.

The English officers repeatedly brought their colors
forward to animate the troops and charged at their
head. But two more barrels of powder exploded among
the English, completely shattering what spirit they had
left. Nothing remained for the royal forces but to hack
their way, every man for himself, out of the slaughter.
The English horse creditably held the ford open for the
foot and protected them all the way back to Armagh.

That night, out of Bagenal's army of 4,350 men, the
remnants of about 1,500 lay cooped up in the Cathe-
dral of Armagh, with the Irish fires winking on the hills
around. Bagenal's corpse lay among them. The army
had been cut to pieces. It had lost all its colors, its cannon, about 20 captains, all its ammunition and food. It
had lost Blackwater fort and the year's fighting. It was
the worst disaster ever suffered by the English in Ireland.

The victory of the Yellow Ford seemed to lay Ireland at Tyrone's feet. Everywhere the patriotic and the
discontented took up arms. By the end of 1598 the
rebel forces had swelled to some 30,000 horse and foot.
Messengers were sent galloping to Dublin for help as
Tyrone's raiders burned to within 12 miles of the Pale.
All over the south settlers were fleeing from their estates into walled cities like Cork and Limerick, leaving
their spoils, arms, and ammunition to the rebels. The
country was said to be "impassable to any faithful sub-

ject, especially those who wear hose and breeches."

Men spoke openly of Tyrone as king of Ireland. His messengers abroad were treated as ambassadors. Philip of Spain wrote a warm letter of congratulation on the success at the Yellow Ford. Some said the pope was having a crown made for the earl's coronation. But on the streets of Dundalk the remark was heard, "The Earl will climb so high as he will break his neck."

With the spread of Tyrone's rebellion, priests were again on the march, binding the broken parts of Irish life into the double crusade—nationalism and religion. The idealism of the Counter Reformation came to dominate Tyrone—once an almost wholly worldly-minded man—until it outweighed every personal and political motive for the war. The religious issue, starting as a mere pennant, became a full-blown banner. Ominously, all Tyrone's oaths were reduced to one—"By this cross on my sword!"

Elizabeth, in a rage after Yellow Ford, loosened her purse strings and launched "the royalest army that ever went out of England"—16,000 foot and 1,500 horse under the command of her favorite, Robert Devereux, earl of Essex. But Essex hated Ireland—that "moist, rotten island." Even as he made his state entry into Dublin on April 15, 1599, surrounded by his gentlemen, all with their short velvet cloaks, great ruffs, and rich swords, his teeth were chattering with Irish ague. The Queen had ordered him to proceed north immediately and attack Tyrone with the full weight of his forces. However, the Council in Dublin induced him to postpone his march to Ulster till the grass had grown and the cattle were fat. He wasted his troops putting down minor insurrections in the south until, four months after taking command, his army of 16,000 had been reduced to 4,000, "the rest either dead, runaway or converted into Irish."

When at last Essex and his dwindled forces came

The Battle of Yellow Ford

face to face with Tyrone, effective action was no longer possible. On September 14, 1599, the two leaders held a parley on horseback at the ford of Annaclint on the border of Monaghan. Tyrone rode into the stream up to his horses' belly as an Irish token of respect. Essex stayed on the bank. The conversation lasted half an hour, and as there were no witnesses it remains one of the enigmas of history. Many believed that the two men plotted to compound forces—Tyrone to back Essex for the English succession after Elizabeth's death. Essex agreed to a six months' truce, dispersed his army, and rushed back to London. But as he met his death by the headsman's axe on February 25, 1600, the mystery of the parley in the Ulster woods remained unsolved.

In the winter of 1599, Tyrone reached the summit of his career. No lord in England or on the Continent was so powerful. The government tried to negotiate but the earl's demands had vaulted. His terms of surrender amounted to "Home Rule" voiced for the first time in Irish history. One of his chief aims was the restoration of Catholic Ireland, but with *freedom of conscience,* almost unheard of in the 16th century with the Inquisition at its height. In London, Lord Cecil, reading Tyrone's demands for Ireland, had smiled and written across the dispatch, "Utopia."

In the spring of 1600, Elizabeth made the supreme effort to crush the Tyrone rebellion. She dispatched an army of 20,000 under Lord Mountjoy, the greatest English soldier of the period. He was no blustering gallant like so many of his predecessors, but a cold, stern, silent man, as relentless as Cromwell in the pursuit of an objective. He proceeded to drive a wedge between Tyrone and his southern chieftains by building a ring of forts around Ulster. Tyrone could not stop him as his allies were falling away in staggering numbers. Each of the many chiefs in the Irish confederation was "king in his own country," and Mountjoy was exploiting their feuds and jealousies, ancient and new, to the utmost. Irish captains sought English bounties, carrying in their fists sackfuls of their brothers' heads.

Aside from defections among his followers, Tyrone was pressed for money. The war was costing him upwards of 4,000 pounds a day, a fantastic outlay for a 16th century chieftain. Then, too, he was in bitter need of Scots—the tall *gallowglasses* who had served Ulster for over three centuries. The English navy was standing guard over the straits, and the Scots, bottled up on their Western Isles, could not cross to Ireland. In the summer of 1600, Tyrone told his confederates in a meeting at Strabane: "I will for one quarter of a year bear up the war, and by that time if things fall not out well, I will exhibit such conditions of peace as I know the English will not reject."

He remained in the field the whole year, hacking away at Mountjoy, but was unable to stop him from pressing up mile-by-mile to the very borders of his deepest fastnesses. All through the war Tyrone had watched for Spanish bearing men and supplies. Only the great trump card of Spanish help would reknit his confederation and give him the decisive victory he needed. Time and again expeditions sailed from Cadiz bound for Ireland, only to be attacked by storms and set on the run by the weather. In August of 1601 the wraith of a Spanish fleet finally materialized, but it landed as far out of Tyrone's reach as possible, on the extreme south of Ireland at Kinsale. If the northern Irish wished to contact these Spanish allies, it meant a forced march in bad weather from tip to toe of the island.

Mountjoy, jubilant over his unexpected advantage, gathered together what forces he could and proceeded to Kinsale. There he bottled up the Spaniards, some 5000 fighting men, behind the walls of the tiny fishing

village before they could get loose in the country. Their
fleet had sailed off and left them so they had no choice
but to submit to the siege and wait to be rescued by
their allies.

It was November before Tyrone broke through the
ring of forts that hemmed him in and started south to
relieve the Spanish. Even then his progress was a
crawl. The Irish marched with a bag of meal and butter on their backs and a pair of brogans, every horse
carrying a spare set of shoes. There were no wagons.
As Tyrone knew, it was a guerrilla army out of its element, untrained for sieges, and altogether unfit for
pitched battle. But the Spaniards had become stinging
in their reproaches and, much against his judgment, he
made the march. As it turned out, it would have been
better if he had stayed home.

On December 8, the English besiegers heard the
deep woods behind their encampment begin to rustle
and they knew the Irish had arrived and were closing
in. Everything was in Tyrone's hands. The enemy was
in open country at the mercy of foul weather. He con-
trolled all the roads over which Mountjoy's supplies
had to travel. Even the wind was anti-English and
would not blow from the east so that ships could bring
victuals from home. Tyrone had only to wait in order
to starve out the English as they had hoped to starve
out the Spanish. He threw away all his advantages
when he decided to attack. At this point one of
Tyrone's commanders ran out of whiskey and sent over
to an officer in the English camp beseeching him for a
bottle. When he received it, he rewarded the donor
with a message giving away the time which had been
set for the joint Irish-Spanish assault.

The night of December 23 was dark and wild, with
lightning flaming like lamps on the lance-heads. Before
dawn Tyrone's guerrillas crept forward in a mass to
within three quarters of a mile of the English encamp-

ment. But Mountjoy, being forewarned, was ready. He sent out two regiments of horse and foot, about 2000 men, to meet the advance. Tyrone retired behind a stream and bog, and there he waited in the breaking dawn. But no stir came from the town. Mountjoy had left half his forces, 4000 men, to meet the Spanish assault and they had apparently given up the idea of making one.

When the English commander learned there was firm, open ground—just what he wanted—beyond the bog where the Irish had taken cover, he marched his foot around to the firm ground at top speed. He was then able to offer full attack from the rear upon Tyrone's center, estimated at 1,800 strong, with both horse and foot. The massed Irish pikemen took the royal charge, held it, turned it, and defeated it.

Mountjoy, watching from a short distance, saw the retreat of his cavalry, and in haste called up all the remaining horse he had. Then all the English horse together fell upon the Irish center, and the flanking Irish cavalry as well. This assault achieved an amazing success. The Irish horse immediately broke and fled; the forest of Irish pikes, opening its ranks to let some of the fleeing horsemen through, was immediately itself pierced and broken. It fled in confusion, pursued by the English cavalry for two miles, hacking and hewing. The battle was over in an hour. The one cavalry charge on open ground saw the end of independent Gaelic Ireland. It was an astonishing termination of a war in which the Irish had won victory after victory.

For Tyrone, "the Victory of Christmas Eve"—as the English called Kinsale—was a debacle. What was left of his army melted away in his long flight back to the north. But he still had the magic of his name—The O'Neill—and no one would betray him. He took refuge in the trackless depths of Glenconkein, there to fight it out to the last, lost, savage glen. But the English kept on tightening with new forts the ring which they had built before Kinsale. Castle Dungannon itself had become an English garrison. Tyrone's lean cattle wandered in search of food where he hid. There were no crops since he could not stay long enough in one place to harvest any. But it was impossible to keep up the hunted life forever, and he had so few men left upon whom he could rely there was no glimmer of hope that his luck would turn.

On March 30, 1603, Tyrone laid down his arms in Dublin and made submission to the queen. Mountjoy did not tell him that Elizabeth had died March 24. If Tyrone had known of her death he would undoubtedly have held out to extract more honorable terms for himself and his confederates from the new King James of Scotland who had always shown him friendship.

With Tyrone's surrender, the last unconquered province of Ireland was thrown open to English law and government. After eight years fighting, 600,000 acres of land belonged to the Ulster chieftains were divided among English colonists. Tyrone was above all else a Gaelic chieftain, and the last peerages of Gaelic blood went down with him. He was permitted to keep the title of earl of Tyrone and those lands which had been his before the rebellion. But he was shorn of all real power. He was forbidden to practice his religion, even in private. He was robbed left and right in fraudulent lawsuits.

He knew his enemies were closing in, so that when a French ship put into Lough Swilly in autumn of 1607, and the captain offered him passage to the Continent, he seized the chance. He made up a small party including his countess, the earl of Tyrconnel, and their close followers. They secretly boarded the ship September 14, 1607, a date that is indelible in Irish history as "The Flight of the Earls."

Tyrone's progress across Europe was an endless

Lord Mountjoy

triumph. In Rome, the pope gave him Salviati Palace
as a residence and pensioned him generously, if for no
other reason than because he had been such a persistent thorn in the side of Protestant Elizabeth. It was a
peaceful epilogue for the grand rebel. But sometimes
as friends gathered in the evening in Salviati Palace,
the aging earl would swear over the wine that he
would yet go back and die in Ireland. The wish was
not granted him. He died in Rome, July 20, 1616, and
was buried with the greatest pomp under the pavement
in the Church of San Pietro de Montoria. There he lies
with his Gaelic captains beside the remains of Dante's
Beatrice.

Prince Charles Edward Stuart

THE VERY SHORT CAREER OF BONNIE PRINCE CHARLIE

By Nancy Anderson

*I*n the fall of 1745, residents of Edinburgh, Scotland, were faced with a familiar yet always cruel problem: Just what should they do about the royalty currently in residence in their city? If they offered further resistance to the young man who had settled in at Holyrood Palace, home of his great-great-great-grandmother, Mary, Queen of Scots, with the pronouncement that his father, James, was now their king, his fearsome Highland followers might extract blood-thirsty vengeance.

On the other hand, if the Edinburghers hurrahed their regal visitor and acknowledged him their lord, the coldly efficient British troops who still held Edinburgh Castle would certainly wreak awful vengeance given half a chance.

English vengeance was nothing new to Edinburghers

who had long since learned that their neighbors to the south considered all Scots, proper townsfolk as well as untamed Highlanders, barbarians deserving scant consideration from civilized men.

But, whether the villagers who dwelt under the shadow of Edinburgh Castle supported or opposed Charles Edward Stuart, the youth who was trying to claim a kingdom, one thing was certain: They could not ignore him.

For Charlie (often called the "bonnie" prince) was not only at home in his ancestral mansion, Holyrood Palace, maintained there by doughty, tartaned clansmen, but he had inherited a bounty of the famous Stuart charm. Charlie was magnetic, and despite the ruffian company he kept, he was as citified as any Edinburgher, for the prince, was a product of Rome and Paris.

On the basis of his charm and successes to the moment it was easy to believe that Bonnie Prince Charlie would secure his hold on Scotland and actually place his doddering father, the Old Chevalier, son of England's rejected James II, on the throne. This was his announced intention. However, while Charlie had inherited the Stuart charm, he had also drawn his share of the Stuarts' fatal lack of common sense, a serious flaw in the family makeup which had made it difficult for crowned heads of that line to keep their crowns.

So Edinburghers, pondering the delightful Charles Edward and his rag-tag army of clansmen, simply didn't know which way to jump to secure their own interests. Thus it had always been.

Throughout their nation's history Scots had killed and been killed due to the general instability of their throne. However, no chapter in Scottish history is more bloody nor tragic and none has had a more lasting effect upon the country than the one which opened with the dream of Bonnie Prince Charlie.

Charles Edward Stuart, the impractical, romantic-minded grandson of the king who'd been James II of England and James VII of Scotland, disposed of his titles in England's Bloodless Revolution. Numerous Scots and others (all called Jacobites) had ardently hoped that this James' son known as James the Pretender, or the Old Chevalier, would eventually be brought to power, and three times they'd thrown their country into civil war for the sake of their expectations. The intrigue and the killing in James' behalf had produced ballads and legends, including the stories of Rob Roy McGregor, but little else.

Now a teutonic cousin of James the Pretender, George II, was on the combined throne of England and Scotland, and a gallant and bonnie visionary, James' son, had come to depose him. That the visionary was also hairbrained, events would unfortunately prove.

No one on either side of the border felt much enthusiasm for George, a plump, phlegmatic man with regal qualities. Nevertheless, a great number of Scots felt no enthusiasm for civil war and preferred life under the dull Hanover to death in the ranks of even the most exciting Stuart. So, when bonnie pretender, Charlie, arrived on their shores, there was no general acclaim for his venture.

Charlie had been reared in Europe and had hoped to secure the backing of France for his gamble. However, the French king, though he cordially loathed England and had gone to war with that country in 1743, declined to commit French might to assist another Stuart Restoration.

Perhaps the Stuart tendency, as displayed by several generations, to mix courage with addle-headedness put him off. At any rate, Charlie was a bold youngster not twenty-five years old who refused to let the French king's disinterest change his plans.

He wrote to his father that he was "determined to

91

conquer or die," and declared, "I will go if I have but a single footman."

In July, 1745, the prince with two ships, an army of seven friends known to romance as "The Seven Men of Moidart," and almost no supplies rashly sailed from France. A British man-o'-war damaged and turned back one ship. Charlie, however, was no more to be dissuaded from his mission than his great-uncle, King Charles II, had been dissuaded from wenching. He landed on the mainland at Lock nan Uamh on July 25 and was promptly warned by a handful of Highland chiefs that he'd better turn around and go back.

By contrast, Catholic Bishop Hugh MacDonald of Morar, stepbrother to the chief of his clan, welcomed Charlie and blessed his standard. Word of this blessing caused some Protestant Scots to twitch, but in the Highlands religion was not often a fighting matter. Some Catholic clans had Protestant chiefs, while some powerful tribes like the Camerons and Stewarts of Appin were Protestant.

The English king (or his representatives) had made some attempt to route Catholicism out of the kingdom but without much success in the sword-held glens of the Highlands. For example, when soldiers of the Hanover George tried to arrest Father John Farquharson in the Chisolm country, his parishioners not only defended him but favored killing the troopers and burying them under the altar. The priest talked his flock out of such unchristian revenge (reminiscent of St. Peter's reaction to the soldiers at Gethsemane), but the father was never harassed by his Protestant sovereign again.

When Prince Charlie sternly told the chiefs who urged him to leave Scotland that he was going to do or die, many Catholic priests "mongst the lochs and the bens" joyously became his recruiting officers. Some even belted on their broadswords and went out with their battle-bound clans as chaplains. In Strathoven Father Grant and Father Tyrie cast lots for the pleasure of going to war. Father Tyrie, the winner, marched off with his sword, dirk, and target while the disappointed Father Grant stayed home to fight less exciting engagements with the devil. Priests, of course, were well and good, but what Charlie really needed beside him were chieftains.

Soon two important clan leaders joined him—young Lochiel, son of the chief of the Camerons, and young MacDonald, son of the chief of the MacDonalds. The MacDonalds were the greatest clan of Scotland incorporating one hundred septs (or subclans). The clan of Donald boasted mighty warriors, too, and had been promised by Robert Bruce himself that whenever he or his descendants went into battle they would stand to the right of the king. The MacDonalds had yielded their place of honor on rare occasions over the years— once to the MacLeans, another clan of powerful warriors—but they only yielded voluntarily as an act of courtesy, not by command.

Others, largely Highland leaders and their men, gave allegiance to the prince until on August 19, less than a month after he landed in Scotland, Charles Edward raised his standard, a gorgeous banner of red and white silk, at Glenfinnian, and his audacious adventure was irrevocably underway.

From this distant time and place, it's hard to pinpoint just why the Highlanders were drawn with such suicidal dedication to Charlie. He was, of course, courageous, and courage is a virtue traditionally esteemed by the Scots. Some may have come, because they, like he, were Catholic, but few would have responded to this impulse, because Catholic clans seldom bothered to war against Protestant neighbors unless something more than faith was involved.

Charles was bonnie, of course, which was much more than one could say for his cousin George. His suit, now displayed in the city museum in Inverness, reveals that he was a well-made young man on the tall side when compared with other men of his day. His hair was reddish like that of the hero-king, Robert Bruce. According to tradition, he had the physical endurance of any mountain-bred clansman, and he relished honor, that intangible of which Highlanders made a fetish. Finally, he was a Stuart, bearing a name which was magic in the northern wildernesses of Scotia.

Bruce's daughter had married a Stewart, thus founding the line, and for four hundred years numerous Highland clans had been emotionally and genealogically connected with the regal strain. The MacLeans of Mull claimed descent from Bruce through his second daughter, while the MacGregors insisted they were a royal race. The Appin Stewarts were vain that they bore the king's name, and on and on the proud assertions went. A waggish visitor to Scotland once remarked, "Two-thirds of these people claim to be kin to the king, and two-thirds of them are."

In the minds of all concerned, friend and foe alike, Prince Charles was descended from Bruce. Whether or not he was heir to Bruce's throne would be settled by claymores and cannon in the months ahead. Some of the Highlanders who flocked to Charlie didn't know what his claim to kingship was and really didn't care because kings carried small weight in their remote, tribal territories.

The clansmen lived under a patriarchal and totally feudal system wherein they owed their lives and loyalty to their chiefs who, in turn, owed them protection. Each clan was bound by common name, common memory of great deeds, common superstitions, and a hair-trigger sense of honor which could explode at an instant into violence.

To the rest of the world, including Lowland Scots, clansmen were wild if not actually mad, for who, other than a madman, would mouth the unchristian-sounding babble which was Gaelic speech? Actually, the Highlanders spoke the same language as the Irish of that day and had strong ties to Ireland, having joined the Irish as allies in various wars. And, in the English view, the Irish connection was one of the blackest marks against the clans, for, to the Sothron, if there was anything more barbarous than a Highlander, it was an Irishman.

Duncan Forbes, laird of Culloden and a supporter of King George, wrote of the clansmen and their country: "What is properly called the Highlands of Scotland is that large tract of mountainous ground on the Northwest of the Tay, where the natives speak the Irish language. The inhabitants stick closely to their antient (sic) and idle way of life; retain their barbarous customs and maxims; depend generally on their chiefs as their Sovereign Lords and masters; and being accustomed to the use of Arms and inured to hard living, are dangerous to the public peace. . . ."

From the peaks and the glens the clansmen came to Charlie, summoned by the burning cross. In the Highlands, warriors were called out when two burning sticks bound to form a cross and tied with linen dipped in goat's blood were carried through the land. Messengers running in relay passed the cross from hand to hand until it had traversed a territory. And in answer every Highland boy old enough to bear arms and every man fit to fight was expected to report for duty, and any who failed his chief would pay dearly. At best, his house would be burned and, at worst, he'd be cast out of his clan, a fate equivalent to that of a Viking warrior dying of the mumps.

The chiefs were the father-figures of their tribes with the power of life and death over their clansmen. They preserved tatters of a warlike and romantic honor to which their followers thoroughly subscribed. The great chiefs sent their sons to be educated on the Continent, often read both Latin and Greek and, when they swore, combined the name of God with a Pantheon of Celtic and Norse deities, for the Western Isles of Scotland had originally been part of the Norse empire, and the seed of Vikings had strengthened the Island tribes.

Some Highlanders pledged their lives to Bonnie Prince Charlie through clan pride or simple loyalty to chiefs. Some were there to continue mountain feuds of earlier vintages. Hatred of the Campbells, for example, helped draw MacDonalds, MacLeans, and Stewarts into the Young Pretender's ranks. One John Roy Stewart had aired his sentiments by composing a parody on the 23rd Psalm: "The Lord is my target (shield). I will be stout with dirk and trusty blade; though Campbells come in flocks about, I will not be afraid." Clan Campbell was famous, powerful, and in the service of King George. Its feud with the MacDonalds was almost as old as time. On general principles, every Campbell was born to war with every MacDonald and vice versa.

The MacLeans, though, could cite specifics against the Campbell clan, for, while MacLean men had been away from their lonely homes, Campbells had raided their country burning houses, stripping women, and stealing cattle.

Soon after Charlie raised his standard at Glenfinnan, he commanded a large enough army to capture Perth, parade through Sterling, and move to the outskirts of Edinburgh.

Meanwhile, the English had placed an army under Sir John Cope and sent it to crush the rebellion. Sir John set out right manfully, but he and Charlie marched right by one another, each innocent of his enemy's whereabouts. Cope drove all the way to Inverness in the heart of the Highlands, while Charlie concentrated on scaring the folk of Edinburgh half to death. When he arrived at a point almost within shouting distance, the city's residents considered resistance. However, when this appeared pointless, they sent a deputation to negotiate. Charlie's terms were simple: invite him and his army into town and have done with the shilly-shallying.

But before the Edinburghers could decide exactly how to respond, nine hundred Highlanders entered the city without waiting for an invitation. A few hours later, Bonnie Prince Charlie moved into Holyrood Palace and proclaimed his father king of Scotland under the name of James VIII. With that out of the way, he extended invitation to a grand ball to be held that night.

Many a pretty Edinburgh girl must have blushed, flushed, and trembled as she laced on her stays in preparation for the party, fearing she'd be asked to dance with the rebel prince, or (oh, horrors!) fearing she wouldn't.

Meanwhile, Cope meandered through Scotland. Eventually he almost caught up with Charlie, but the dashing Pretender didn't wait for that to happen. He moved to meet the English at Prestonpans, surprised them there, and almost destroyed them. Then he returned to Edinburgh where he settled down as virtual master of Scotland. Of course, the English still held Edinburgh Castle from which they occasionally, almost absent-mindedly, fired a cannon.

But Charlie's council was meeting regularly at Holyrood as though there weren't an Englishman for miles, and there was even talk of convening a Scottish parliament. If Charles had been content to wait quietly for further developments, perhaps he could have lived out his life in Edinburgh. Or if he'd moved more quickly, he might have scored a further coup. But now the traditional Stuart tendency to make the wrong move at the wrong time manifested itself, and Charlie, after much waiting, decided to conquer England.

He hoped that numerous English would rise to his support and, acting on this theory, sent a team of recruiters, a whore, and a drummer boy into Manchester ahead of him. Their combined efforts produced only two hundred men, and these may have been more intent upon following the whore than upon following Charlie.

Nevertheless, on November 3, 1745, the Pretender with six thousand men and five hundred cavalry began his invasion of the South. Almost no volunteers joined his ranks, and some Highlanders exercising their unpredictable individuality left for home.

By December 4, Charlie was at Derby, only 127 miles from London, and George was seriously thinking of flight to Germany. However, the Pretender didn't know this, nor did he know that the Jacobites of Wales were planning an uprising for December 8 in support of his cause. But he did know that his supply lines were stretched too long and that his men were discouraged. So on December 6, a day remembered as "Black Friday," the chagrined Charles Edward Stuart ordered a retreat to Scotland.

Lord George Murray, a seasoned soldier who had been "out in the Rising of '15" and who may have had the best tactical mind in Charlie's army, directed the retreat with enormous skill.

By this time Edinburgh was firmly in English hands, so the Pretender and his Highlanders headed for Stirling. Here they received reinforcements, Mackintosh clansmen, rallied and dispatched by a remarkable young beauty named Anne.

Like brave Lady Isabel Buchan who defied her husband years before to crown Robert Bruce, king of Scotland, Lady Mackintosh was defying her husband when she threw support to Charlie. Anne was twenty years old and the cousin of Lord George Murray. Her husband had marched away to serve as an officer in King George's army which must have suited her well, for, with him out of the way, she induced the remaining men of Clan Mackintosh to come out for the prince. "Colonel" Anne, as she came to be known, presented each of her recruits with a white cockade as he left for war and then, donning a man's blue bonnet and a tartan, rode to the head of their line and led them to the Pretender. Since Anne was a brave and attractive girl of twenty and Charles was a brave and "bonnie" man of twenty-five, it's nice to speculate upon their private conversations.

Because Charlie's later life was to be so drab and unrewarding, it would be nice to say with certainty that he and Anne enjoyed a brief but blissful idyll in the dream-shrouded Highlands, but unhappily there is no proof. Nevertheless, in February of 1746, with the enemy all about him, Charlie and a few of his men became houseguests at Moyhall, invited there by its mistress, Lady Mackintosh.

The Hanoverians, close by in Inverness, hearing that their royal prey was close at hand, dispatched 1,500 men to seize him. Luckily for Charles, a friend in Inverness got wind of English intentions and sent a boy to Moyhall to warn him. Charles slipped away to safety; however, thanks to his former hostess, "Colonel" Anne, the English march to Moyhall wasn't uneventful. Lady Mackintosh, thinking of the prince's safety, had posted a handful of men on the road from Inverness to serve as lookouts.

When they saw King George's men approach, they raised the war-cries of various clans and fired their guns in all directions so that the English thought they'd been surprised by an entire Highland army. The English fled madly in what came to be known as "The Rout of Moy." The only man killed in the engagement was a piper in the advance guard (for some Scots were serv-

ing with the English), Donald Ban McCrimmon, Mac-
Leod's piper from Skye.

The English evacuated Culloden leaving the town to
Charlie who enjoyed a seven week respite from crisis.
While his troops prowled over the countryside fighting
skirmishes here and there, the Young Pretender divided
his time between Culloden House and Castlehill, both
outside Inverness, and the townhouse of Lady Drum-
muir who was Lady Mackintosh's mother-in-law.

Meanwhile, Charles was falling more and more
under the influence of a man whose intentions were
good but whose notions couldn't have been worse,
Quartermaster General John William O'Sullivan, an
Irishman. Irish troops were part of the Jacobite army,
and, true to their heritage, fought fanatically. However,
some of their countrymen were poor tacticians, notably
General O'Sullivan. Though the Irish and the Scotch
spoke the same language, they used it differently, and
the prince found the Irish gift for poetic flattery especially soothing when compared to the candid address of
the Scots.

More and more he came to rely upon the advice of
Irish friends like Thomas Sheridan, an ancient tutor
who hadn't seen a battle in fifty-six years, and O'Sullivan who, when overwrought, took to his bed for a
bleeding.

Lord George Murray, that wise, old Scottish man at
arms, considered O'Sullivan a nitwit, suggesting that he
was more at home in nightgown and nightcap than in
the paraphernalia of war.

In succumbing to Irish flattery while misjudging the
qualities of men, Charlie exhibited a tragic Stuart tendency. Various of his ancestors, most particularly Mary,
Queen of Scots, had been irresistibly drawn to the
wrong people to their own great detriment.

Meanwhile, a new commander had taken charge of
the English forces, Charles' cousin, the duke of Cum-

berland. William, the duke, was King George's son, a plump, unprepossessing fellow who physically was as unlike Charles as possible.

On the other hand, the two had important qualities in common. First, they were the same age, twenty-five years old, with Charles the elder by four months. Further, each was courageous and attractive to the men he led. Charlie's soldiers called him "bonnie" and admired him for his gaiety, wit, and boldness. William's soldiers admired him only for his boldness, for he was neither witty, bonnie, nor gay. He did establish a small reputation for compassion when, in celebration of his twenty-fifth birthday, he ordered that a seventeen-year-old boy who had been hanging for ten minutes be cut down from the gallows and revived if possible. The youth, suspected of being a rebel spy, was still alive when lowered to the ground but was, according to one of Cumberland's soldiers, "much disordered."

William, however, was not a compassionate man as future events would prove. Shortly he would become known as "The Butcher." The duke celebrated his birthday at Nairn, a Highland village only ten miles from Inverness where his cousin had been resting.

Charlie, aware that a great army was close by, assembled all his available men in Inverness and sent couriers to round up detachments astray in the vicinity. On April 14, 1746, the day that Cumberland and his men reached Nairn, Charles moved his troops to the grounds of Culloden House, but, like a true Stuart, he bumbled. For some reason, when the Highland army moved out, its food and supplies were left behind.

The Jacobites spent April 15 awaiting an attack, but none came. So, in the late afternoon, the Pretender decided to attack the English, taking them by surprise after a night march to Nairn.

Lord George was annoyed with his leader. The prince had spent the night before in foolish and boast-

*The first meeting of Prince Charles
with Flora MacDonald*

ful conversation with his Irish officers and seemed to have a poor grasp of the realities of the situation. When Charlie proposed that they attack the English the next morning, Lord George demurred, recommending, instead, an attack that very night.

The old soldier was worried, for he knew that the Highlanders were seriously under strength. Groups had dribbled away to protect their home territories from Campbells or to attend to other business, while recruits which had been mustered to fight for Charlie hadn't appeared. The MacPhersons and the Frasers were on their way, but they hadn't reached Inverness.

Nevertheless, the Jacobites began their march to Nairn with Lord George setting a good pace. They were hungry and tired and got lost in the fog and quagmires. Then, during rest-halts, O'Sullivan and Lord George pursued their bitter bickering. The ten mile trek was so badly botched that dawn broke before the Jacobites reached Nairn.

Since surprise was now out of the question, officers ordered a retreat which the prince considered a personal betrayal by Lord George. Back on Culloden moor after a night of marching and no sleep, the clansmen were even hungrier than they'd been the day before.

At Culloden House, a servant offered Charlie a nice meal of roast lamb and fowls which certainly tempted the young man, since he was just as hungry as his soldiers. But Charlie, displaying another Stuart trait, a knack for certain grandeur, refused the feast saying, "I cannot eat while my men are starving."

When the prince appeared on the moor, he was haggard from lack of sleep, for, during the two hours after the army's return from Nairn, he had ridden into Inverness in hopes of finding food for his warriors.

"Go on, my lads," he called to the troops standing ready to receive an attack. "The day will be ours."

Lord George continued to fret, for he disliked the

moor Charles had chosen to defend. Of it he later said, "I did not like the ground. It was certainly not proper for Highlanders." However it had been selected by O'Sullivan, Charlie's incompetent favorite.

The MacDonalds weren't happy either, for they had been placed on the left of the line, their traditional place of honor to the right being held by the Athollmen. But the die was cast, so here, on a moor ideal for an English cavalry attack but all wrong for Highland infantrymen, the clansmen made their stand.

At eleven o'clock in the morning, Cumberland appeared leading about nine thousand men including eight hundred mounted dragoons. The duke would never win another battle, but at Culloden he deployed his forces with skill. Then he took his place on horseback behind the front line and to the right.

While Charlie counted approximately eight thousand in his army, only about five thousand were present at Culloden, since others were away scouring for food, guarding passes, sleeping, or wondering what was going on, having failed to get word that a battle was shaping. The prince had scant artillery and almost no trained gunners. In his "Plan of the Battle," John Finlayson, who was master of ordnance, showed only nine Jacobite guns at Culloden.

Fighting began at about one o'clock with Charlie badly mismanaging his part of it. Apparently he wanted Cumberland's men to charge first, so he held his Highlanders in line while English guns cut them to bits.

The clansmen were hard to control. With superhuman courage they took the fire for as long as (according to some authorities) twenty minutes. Despairing, they begged for orders to charge until Lord George sent a message to the prince urging him to launch his attack. At last, Charlie agreed, but the courier carrying the order to the front was killed by a cannonball before he delivered the message.

English cannon roared, clansmen fell, until, at last, the Mackintoshes who'd marched to Charlie with white cockades in their bonnets could stand it no more. Roaring their battle cry, *"Loch Moy,"* they charged carrying the right wing of the Jacobite line with them.

All was confusion. Clansmen broke through the Hanoverian line, but, in the face of so much fire and steel, couldn't sustain their attack.

Highland pipes ranted, driving the Scots to suicidal courage. From the English side, Campbell pipes answered adding to the Jacobites' rage.

All along the line, left as well as right, the clansmen charged. Lord George's horse bolted, carrying him completely through the enemy line where the doughty Scotsman lost his hat and wig and broke his sword. Amazingly, he fought his way back to the protection of the Camerons and Stewarts.

The hair-brained O'Sullivan, of course, continued to contribute to the disasters of the day. First, before the battle began, he neglected to tear down a stone wall which later greatly complicated the Highlanders' plight. Next he placed the men in ranks of six rather than ranks of three so that, during the cannonading, a ball passing through one clansman was likely to kill five more.

In the last agonizing moments of the battle when the Jacobite cause was dead and its supporters dying, O'Sullivan could only exclaim, "All is going to pot."

Culloden produced incidents of personal valor which have been preserved in the Scots' national lore. After seventeen Ardshiel Stewarts sacrificed themselves trying to save their banner, a Morvern man named Domhnull Molach (Hairy Donald) cut the flag from its staff and escaped with it wrapped around his body. It's now displayed in the Scottish United Services Museum in Edinburgh.

A MacGilivray, Robert Mor, lost his weapons but

broke off a peat cart shaft with which he killed seven redcoats before being killed himself.

The Irish Jacobites gallantly covered the retreat allowing the remnants of Clan MacDonald to escape from the field.

When the battle, which lasted scarcely more than an hour, was over, the English cheered Cumberland. As the Jacobites retreated, English dragoons pursued cutting down civilians as well as soldiers. A man plowing near Leys Castle and his nine-year-old son were among the victims. But killing wasn't enough for the victors who obscenely mutilated the dead.

Cumberland gave no quarter, much less medical attention, to the wounded Jacobites. It's told that the duke, riding over the field, came upon a desperately wounded man and asked him to which side he belonged.

"To the Prince," the Highlander, Charles Fraser of Inverallochy, said.

The duke ordered his aide, Brevet-Major James Wolfe, to kill "the insolent rebel" on the spot, but Wolfe refused. So a private soldier carried out the command. This episode, legend says, accounted for Wolfe's later popularity with Highland regiments in Canada. The story is probably a fable, because Wolfe, in his own letters, expressed satisfaction at the slaughter of the clansmen.

Relentlessly Cumberland's men hunted down survivors and their sympathizers. Two days after the battle ended, more than thirty Jacobites found hiding in a barn were burned to death.

Under Cumberland's direction or thanks to his indifference atrocity followed atrocity. In Inverness, a servant girl named Ann MacKay was imprisoned in a cell no larger than a coffin, because she'd helped a prisoner to escape.

Naturally "Colonel" Anne Mackintosh was arrested

and jailed. When one of his officers observed that she was a lady, her captor, Major-General Henry Hawley, answered in that case that he'd hang her upon a mahogany gallows with a silken cord.

He was denied this pleasure.

Actually Anne was accorded better treatment than most Jacobite prisoners and, for a time at least, was issued as much bread as she might request. Since the deliberate policy of the victors was to starve their prisoners, Lady Mackintosh distributed the loaves which were granted her among less fortunate captives and, in this way, probably saved several lives.

There must have been some gallantry within the duke of Cumberland, for only two years after her arrest Anne was not only free but was received in London with considerable acclaim. She was "caressed by Ladys of Quality" (not that Anne would have like that too well), was "favorably received by the Publick," and was even invited to a ball given by the "Butcher" himself. According to one legend, Cumberland insisted that Colonel Anne be his dancing partner, and she, agreeing, asked if she might call the tune. The duke graciously consented whereupon Lady Mackintosh demanded that the musicians play, "The Auld Stuarts Back Again," a tune celebrating the claims of her lost prince. It's to William's credit that, like a good soldier, he bravely tread the measure to the distasteful strain.

Or, at least, that's how the story goes.

Anne returned to the Highlands and apparently to her husband's bed. In 1763, she was elected a Burgess Freewoman and Guild Sister of the Brugh of Inverness, and after her husband's death in 1770 she became housekeeper and hostess for his nephew, the twenty-third chief of the clan.

Anne had only one child, a daughter who died in infancy and is buried at Moy. Later Anne may have lived for a while with her brother, James Farquharson, at Invercauld. She died in 1787 at Leith and was buried in a cemetery there which has been all but obliterated by a railway.

The youngest prisoner taken after Culloden was eight years old, and the oldest eighty. Through Cumberland's vengeance, more than three thousand Scots disappeared through execution, death in prison, or transportation to the Colonies as slaves.

Since the duke of Cumberland was convinced that "this generation (of Scots) must be pretty well wore out" before rebellions would end, he proceeded to wear it out with "the harrying of the glens." His officers moved across the Highlands carrying fire and sword exterminating people, some of whom had never heard of Prince Charles.

An English soldier, surveying his nation's handiwork, complacently wrote, "For the space of Fifth Miles, neither House, Man nor Beast was seen."

Throughout northern Scotland, organized robbery and murder prevailed. Scots who managed to stay alive did so by hiding in caves, and among the Jacobites hiding in the hills was Prince Charles himself. Charlie had remained on the battlefield until the end. Reportedly, when the last of his men were in flight, he offered to lead them on foot in one more suicidal charge. His friends couldn't permit this and, instead, dragged him off the field and into hiding. For five months, he hid among the Scots, and despite a thirty thousand pound reward for his capture, no one betrayed him.

For a time, he was sheltered by "The Seven Men of Glenmoriston," seven folk heroes, who vowed never to surrender and never to end their war against the English. Operating as guerrillas, they plagued the English long after Culloden. It's uncertain what happened to six of them, but one eventually joined King Georges' army and served with a Highland regiment in Canada.

Charlie's escape from Scotland was affected by an

The Battle of Culloden, April 16, 1746

*The Duke of Cumberland
chasing rebels in Scotland*

imaginative and valiant girl named Flora MacDonald who disguised him as her serving woman and spirited him to the Isle of Skye from whence he sailed to France.

Soon he was no longer bonnie. His hope was gone, but he tried pitifully to revive it through drink. The gallant and magnetic prince became a dissolute and embarrassing old man. He'd been born with the graces which marked the Royal Scottish Line, the House of Stuart, but also with the failings, and the latter struck him down.

Flora MacDonald paid for her devotion to Charlie with imprisonment in the Tower of London. However, she was eventually freed, married, and moved to North Carolina where a women's college was named in her honor.

The English parliament debated sterilizing all Jacobite women and destroying all seed corn and farm implements in Scotland "so to extirpate the inhabitants of the cursed country." The laws eventually passed were less drastic than some of the proposals, but they stilled the heart of the Highlands. The wearing of kilts and tartans was forbidden as was carrying and playing bagpipes. Severe restrictions were placed upon Catholics, and Episcopalians were also restricted in their worship. Other laws were designed to break up the clans and obliterate the social and political systems of the country.

Nearly thirty years after Culloden, Dr. Samuel Johnson journeyed through the Highlands and was moved to quote Tacitus: "They have created a desert and have called it peace."

After Culloden, half of a nation, Scotland, was ravaged so thoroughly that the country has never fully recovered from the ordeal. Yet some positive results came from William's revenge. Tough Highlanders who otherwise would have strengthened their native land fled or were transported to the New World where their hardihood, resourcefulness, and sense of honor helped create the United States and Canada.

And how shall we judge Bonnie Prince Charlie? He left desolation behind him on the glens and the moors, but he also left a romantic legend which shines prettily in the memory of man. Practicality never guided Charlie so much as ideals. He dared the impossible through principle, driven by virtue and not expediency. Yet in a pragmatic world he almost became a king.

Field Marshall Wellesley,
Duke of Wellington

A LONG
AND BLOODY WAR

By Richard L. Blanco

*T*he furious rebellion of Madrid's population in May, 1808, against the French Army's occupation of Spain was the spark that flamed a vast insurrection that swept across the entire Iberian Peninsula. In a mass resistance movement that amazed Europe, the Spanish and Portuguese peoples defiantly battled the Napoleonic conquerors in a titanic struggle unmatched until the 20th century in scope, duration, and brutality.

The quixotic insurrection of Spain and Portugal against overwhelming odds impeded the French invasion of Iberia, hampered Napoleon Bonaparte's schemes of domination, and led his supposedly invincible army to defeat. This unexpected uprising, Napoleon's "Spanish Ulcer" which bled away the foundations of his empire, was the first nationalistic upheaval against French tyranny and the first example of total war in modern history. The War of Independence became the testing ground for guerrilla warfare as the battered armies and partisan bands of Spain and Portugal fought a merciless and passionate crusade against Bonaparte's legions.

This bitter contest inspired heretofore subservient nationalities throughout Europe to emulate this dramatic struggle against the French hegemony and it provided Great Britain with a military foothold in Napoleon's Europe. Humiliated by superior French armies since 1793, England secured a strategic front in Portugal under her greatest soldier, Arthur Wellesley, the future duke of Wellington. The Allied dream of defeating Bonaparte became a reality under Wellesley, who with Spanish and Portuguese support campaigned against Napoleon's greatest generals for six years from Lisbon to the Pyrenees.

The Napoleonic Empire was the conservative consolidation of the French Revolution which erupted upon a stunned Europe in 1789. The Revolution became the basis for a remarkable transformation of France's legal, political, and cultural institutions that inspired liberals throughout the Atlantic world. But so rapid and radical were the vast changes emanating from the Parisian upheaval that Europe's reactionary monarchs, huddling together in fear of this ideological torrent that threatened the stability of the old regime, formed successive military coalitions to smother the Revolution in its cradle.

French armies, however, utilizing new tactics and animated by fiery patriotism, hurled back the invaders and annexed satellite states to the triumphant French Republic. With the army acting as the revolutionary spearhead, French Jacobins attempted to bestow on conquered territories the benefits of their own enlightened society dedicated to liberty, equality, and fraternity. Yet whatever the political form of the Revolution, as a Republic, as a Directory, or by 1800 as a Consulate under General Bonaparte, there was no permanent peace. The amazing Corsican, whose quest for glory continued unabated, became emperor of France in 1804 and Europe's New Caesar.

As the French hegemony expanded over the Continent, Napoleon promoted the emergence of a modern Europe unified by rational laws, progressive administrations, and talented technicians. But the empire by 1807 exemplified a virtual betrayal of the Revolution, for France's greatest warrior after his innumerable military and diplomatic victories became a despot. As Napoleon hastily swept away the debris of the old regime, his passion for conformity, rationality, and centralization was increasingly resisted by a Europe that craved an end to the French emperies. And that part of his conquest most defiant of Napoleon was Spain and Portugal, regarded by the haughty emperor as the most backward and priest-ridden in Europe. It was in the Peninsula that Napoleon's splendid army, the key to his success and power, would meet a series of defeats by illiterate peasants crying "King, Church and Independence" in a xenophobic outburst that would baffle the French.

Bonaparte inherited an army in 1800 superior to any European military force, for since the late 18th century significant reforms had occurred in tactics, training, and organization so that French divisions had a degree of morale, mobility, and effectiveness unprecedented in warfare. As a result of her vast resources, her large population (greater than that of Austria, England, and Prussia combined), her stress on national mobilization, mass conscription, and popular propaganda, France astounded Europe in 1794 by maintaining one million troops dedicated to erasing the injustices of the old regime.

The element needed to perfect this military machine was a commander willing to abandon conventional theory and practice of war. In Napoleon, France found her sword. He maneuvered to smash enemy armies separately, attacked unexpectedly, screened his movements by weather and terrain, dispensed with burdensome siege and supply trains, and pushed his devoted soldiers to inhuman limits. In his magnificent victories from Alpine mountains to Egyptian deserts, fighting a larger array of opponents under a greater variety of conditions than any other general in modern history, Napoleon revolutionized the conduct of war.

Although Napoleon's use of cavalry was traditional, in his novel massing of artillery batteries he repeatedly disconcerted his military enemies. With a high ratio of artillery to troops (4-5 guns per 1,000 men compared to the British standard of 1-2 guns), with a concentration of firepower at a target from a number of angles, with increased mobility of cannon units because of sturdy horse-drawn carriages, Napoleon forecast the role of the big gun in the artillery duels of World War I.

In his handling of infantry, the true "Queen of Battle" in the Peninsular War, Napoleon made another great contribution to modern army tactics. French infantry changed from a marching column to a massed, charging column with a speed and precision that awed the frightened enemy deployed in the traditional formation of three straight ranks. As his surging columns were hurled at the foe, Napoleon protected his regiments by intensive artillery bombardments of the opponent, while screens of skirmishers and light infantry cowering behind natural cover decimated the still erect enemy line with lethal hail. Before the startled enemy musketeers could re-form, Napoleon thrust his massed columns into the wavering enemy ranks. Then at the exact moment when the opponent's line cracked the towering Imperial Guards pressed forward, the heavy

Napoleon in Spain

cavalry with sabers and lances charged at an exposed gap, and on the open flanks the light cavalry completed the slaughter.

With a vigorous screening of officers, a ruthless sacrifice of men, and a speed of operations never before witnessed on battlefields, Napoleon had seemingly endless success in humbling Europe's proud dynasties. With the merging of divisions into army corps the emperor brought the army to a peak of efficiency. The marshal's coveted baton that theoretically was in every soldier's knapsack was inducement for incredible feats of daring. With the Legion of Honor bestowed upon the bravest of the brave, Napoleon could justifiably claim that he had "ennobled all Frenchmen."

There were nonetheless profound weaknesses in the French army. Only two thirds of the troops by 1812 were French. Because of nepotism, corruption, and Napoleon's tyranny the army could lose much of its revolutionary zeal. Although the practice of having soldiers forage for their own supplies functioned effectively in the relatively rich agricultural areas and numerous populated cities of Northern Europe, much of the Peninsula was barren and sparse, urban areas were often far apart, and the mountainous terrain could impede the army's mobility.

Napoleon's armies could not stand still on a campaign, for a corps quickly denuded an area of provisions and had to keep constantly in motion. Under certain conditions, reasoned Sir Arthur Wellesley returning to London in 1805 after seven years of military duty in India, a Napoleonic army corps could deteriorate in hostile country, and the French blue column could be defeated by the traditional British line of redcoats.

Yet these defects in the Napoleonic juggernaut were not apparent when the emperor obliterated the Third Coalition by defeating the Austrians at Ulm and Aus-

Wellington in Spain

terlitz (1805), the Prussians at Jena (1806), and the Prussians again and the Russians at Eylau and Friedland (1807). By forcing the Russian Tsar Alexander I to accept the Treaty of Tilsit (July, 1807), Napoleon imposed his peace on Europe.

Yet some national states still eluded France's warlord. Britain, repeatedly rejected from the Continent by French armies, was still defiant. After successive naval victories from 1797 to 1805 climaxed by the triumph at Trafalgar, England mocked Napoleon's plans for a channel invasion. But Napoleon planned to bring the stubborn British to their knees by massive economic warfare, a boycott by Europe of British commerce—the Continental System.

The only front door to Europe not coerced into cooperation with France was weak Portugal. To bully the frightened Braganza dynasty in Lisbon with a minimum of military effort, the emperor considered a tightening of his alliance with the Bourbon regime in Madrid and he pondered whether Spain, supposedly the most ill-governed kingdom of Europe, was ripe for Napoleonic reforms.

And how could Spain refuse to cooperate? Once the dominant nation in Europe under Philip II, the world's leading colonizer, and still the bastion of Catholic orthodoxy, Spain since the 17th century had declined in power and prestige. In the late 18th century, however, as a result of the capable Charles III and his energetic ministers a significant series of reforms occurred so that proud Spain seemed by 1789 on the verge of a vast national regeneration. But the Peninsula had a medieval social structure, antiquated laws, a stagnant economy, and a conservative church clinging to its Inquisition. Spain as well as Portugal was still wrapped in the cloak of parochialism and was immune from the fresh current of the Enlightenment.

A political deterioration began in Spain in the 1790's

under the bumbling Charles IV who was unable to cope with revolutionary forces. His queen, the ugly Maria Louisa, was surely no object of veneration, for as Napoleon commented in disgust she "has her heart and her past on her face." This shabby royal couple was dominated by Manuel Godoy, rumored to be the queen's lover, who as prime minister had ruled almost continually since 1792. Godoy was hailed by the crown as the savior of the monarchy in a turbulent era, but he was bitterly hated by Spanish society.

The scandal and corruption at the Bourbon court, the decline in Spain's influence, the loss of her fleet, the cession of territory (Trinidad, Santa Domingo, Louisiana) because of Spanish involvement in French wars since 1793 created increasing disenchantment for the royal household and Godoy was blamed for every major national disaster since the French Revolution. The great hope for a demoralized Spain in the popular mind was Ferdinand, prince of Asturias and heir to the throne, who as "the desired one" became the symbol of hope and justice for a potentially rejuvenated Spain. Ferdinand, a bitter foe of Godoy, plotted to curtail the minister's influence and to eject his own parents from the Bourbon throne.

In such a decadent setting of intrigue, Napoleon relished the opportunity to become the arbiter of Spain's destiny as the desperate Godoy and the scheming Ferdinand both competed for the emperor's favor. The diplomatic wedge for Napoleon's intervention in the Peninsula came in October, 1807, when Godoy stupidly signed the Treaty of Fontainebleau. This agreement provided for the joint invasion and occupation of Portugal by French and Spanish troops, for the passage of a French army over the Pyrenees, and for the partition of the Braganza kingdom between France and Spain.

Now a French army of 20,000 poised on the Pyrenees hurried to invade Portugal in November, as Napoleon wrote to his marshal, Andoche Junot, that "Lisbon is everything." Under the arrangement with Godoy, Napoleon held another army near Bayonne, France, to ward off a possible British defense of Portugal. But without informing Madrid Napoleon dispatched General Pierre Dupont in December to occupy a strategic chain of Spanish cities in Navarre, Aragon, and Old Castile. To the astonishment of the startled Basques in January, 1808, another 300,000 troops under Marshal Bon Adrien Moncey marched through their provinces. In February, General Pierre Duhesme proceeded through Catalonia to occupy Barcelona and General Jean Baptiste Bessieres followed with another 30,000 men. Thus, with Portugal nearly conquered by Junot, Napoleon by March, 1808, had over 100,000 soldiers in the Peninsula without encountering Spanish military resistance.

After pondering various alternatives to outright annexation of Spain, Napoleon decided in February "that it is necessary to shake up this power which is useless to the general interest." Still masking his intentions from the Bourbons Napoleon determined to extend his occupation of Spain, to send Marshal Joachim Murat to Madrid, to force the entire royal family to abdicate, and to place his brother Joseph Bonaparte on the Spanish throne.

The emperor assumed the potential support of a large urban and professional group of Francophiles along with a national willingness to accept the Napoleonic Code, the secularization of the church, and the abolition of feudalism. But he had not sensed that if the Bourbon dynasty and the Catholic faith seemed in danger to the Spanish populace, the tension rising from months of uncertainty could explode.

As the occupation proceeded there was bewilderment in Madrid over Napoleon's motives. The frightened court gave no leadership, Spanish political and intellectual leaders were perplexed, and many commoners assumed that Napoleon was intervening to displace the hated Godoy and to assist their beloved Ferdinand.

Although there were numerous "incidents" in the smoldering relations between French soldiers and Spanish civilians, the first definitive sign of national unrest occurred on March 17, at the royal residence of Arnajuez. Here, rioting mobs, instigated by Ferdinand's supporters, forced Godoy to resign. Then the terrified King Charles abdicated in favor of his son, Ferdinand, who was proclaimed Spain's new sovereign.

Ferdinand, however, needed Napoleon's diplomatic recognition. Assured by Murat that such support would be forthcoming after discussions with the emperor, the duped Ferdinand traveled north in April with a French escort to the trap at Bayonne. At the same time, Charles, Maria Luisa, and Godoy, all anxious to find sanctuary in France, accepted Napoleon's offer to confer in Bayonne. After amusing himself until early May with the ludicrous spectacle of the quarreling royal mice, Napoleon suddenly pounced and forced them all to abdicate.

The Spanish people were puzzled by the still unreported events at Bayonne, Spain's wretched army was scattered throughout the provinces, and many of her leaders seemed willing to accept the Napoleonic conquest. But the tension was rising in the nation over the arrogant behavior of French troops, at the ineffectiveness of government, and at the lack of direction from any privileged class in the emergency. Only a spark was needed to ignite the burning hatred for the alien French and the incident occurred on May 2.

As Murat prepared to exile the last two members of the royal family to France, city crowds seething with excitement erupted in furious indignation. Seizing any weapon to kill the French, the *madrilenos* strove to drive the invaders from their city and futilely hurled

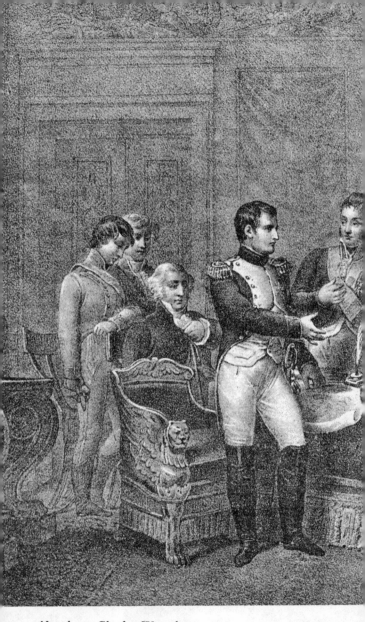

Napoleon, Charles IV and Ferdinand VII at Bayonne

bricks and tiles at Murat's crack infantry and Polish Lancers. Although the bloody fighting was quelled within a few hours, Murat ordered a mass execution of civilians and hundreds of victims were butchered without trial in Madrid's streets.

Now the entire nation exploded into a vast xenophobic outburst as the news of the Madrid massacre and of Ferdinand's abdication spread rapidly to every hamlet. Generals Joaquin Blake, Xavier de Castanos, and Gregoria de la Cuesta mustered their troops, thousands of volunteers flocked to join the Spanish army, regional governments (*juntas*) mobilized for war, and rural priests urged the faithful to defy the atheistic French. By late May Spanish provinces unoccupied by the French were in open rebellion and by early June delegates from Asturias and Galicia were in London begging for muskets.

From Burgos to Seville, from La Coruna to Barcelona, Spain was in arms proclaiming loyalty to her cherished institutions. Just as Joseph Bonaparte was being proclaimed King of Spain in Bayonne to the applause of Spanish collaborators, the Supreme Junta, the provisional government in Aranjuez, declared that "Napoleon will trample down our Monarchy, our Fundamental Laws, and bring about the ruin of our Holy Catholic Religion."

From Galicia on July 16 came this defiant proclamation: "Spaniards! You have no alternative. You must fight bravely for our independence." The citizens' council in Oviedo, Asturias, announced: "Let every man rise in defense of his country . . . Let the population become an armed cap." As indicative of Spanish clerical reaction, the *Times* of London reported that the Bishop of St. Andero "was at the head of insurgents in Asturias . . . with the sword in one hand and the cross in the other."

But the French *blitzkreig* smashed the Spanish armies in the northern provinces. Such cities as Cabezon and Torquemada in Old Castile fell to the invaders by late June, Santander on the Bay of Biscay toppled, and in Navarre, Spanish forces were annihilated in three battles. At some points, however, the French were repulsed. In Aragon, the medieval walled city of Zaragoza withstood a brutal siege, the bastion of Gerona in Catalonia threw back French attacks, and at Valencia, Marshal Moncey and 8,000 veterans, unprepared for the fierce resistance, retreated.

The turning point in the initial fighting came when Bessieres crushed the Spanish forces under Blake and Cuesta at Medina de Rioseco in Valladolid. Now the road to Madrid was open for King Joseph to travel in triumph. Yet, "the fact is," wailed Joseph to Napoleon as he passed through silent streets, "not a single Spaniard is on my side . . ."

However overwhelming were the French victories over the battered Spanish armies, there was one magnificent event, one of the great moments in Spanish history—the triumph at Bailen. General Dupont and 13,000 troops left Toledo in late May on a 300 mile southerly march through La Mancha and Andalucia to capture the vital Atlantic seaport of Cadiz. After crossing the Sierra Morena mountains and pillaging Cordoba, Dupont discovered that his communications to the north were cut and that Andalucia was mobilizing a large army to encircle him.

Expecting General Vedel and 7,000 men from Toledo to reinforce him, Dupont withdrew to the village of Andujar on the Guadalquivir River by mid-June instead of retiring to the more defensible town of Bailen on the road back to the mountains. Dupont's units were scattered, his army stricken with heat, hunger, and sickness, Vedel delayed in supporting him, and the Spanish seized Bailen and the route back to safety. In a panic as 34,000 infuriated Andalucians closed in, Du-

The Battle of Sommo-Sierra, October, 1808

pont tried to ram his exhausted troops through the defenses of Bailen in five desperate assaults. Trapped in open country and surrounded by a determined enemy, Dupont capitulated on July 22 to the victorious Spanish.

Thus, with 2,400 casualties an entire French army of 17,000 effectives surrendered. The defeat at Bailen humiliated the French marshals and it cast doubts about Napoleon's military infallibility. "Bailen" became the great rallying cry for thousands of Spanish troops and scores of guerrilla bands. The news of Bailen was cheered by the valiant Aragonese in besieged Zaragoza, and in London the *Times* reported that the announcement of Bailen "thoroughly convulsed with joy" the British capital.

By September, the supposedly typical Napoleonic conquest became an unprecedented French retreat as the invaders, stunned by the furious defiance, withdrew to the Ebro River where Joseph, fleeing Madrid on August 1, prepared to hold the line. During the bloody summer of 1808 the French lost over 40,000 men, a number of casualties greater than those in six years of future campaigning in the Peninsula against the British. Napoleon held only Burgos, Barcelona, and a string of citadels along the Ebro. Now England had her long awaited chance to strike a blow at Bonaparte and to land an expeditionary force on the mainland.

How ready was England to assist her beleaguered Spanish and Portuguese allies? The record of the British army since 1793 against the French was deplorable, and in an era when battles usually determined the future of nations Britain had consistently failed to influence major diplomatic settlements on the Continent. The decade of peace after the fiascos of Saratoga and Yorktown, the degree of corruption and inefficiency in administration, the attitudes of unimaginative generals still mentally shackled by outmoded military concepts left the army unprepared to challenge the aggressive

French legions.

With ranks filled with degenerates of society, training of engineers and artillerymen was virtually ignored, siege trains and commissary units were existent only on paper; the army was unfit to defy Napoleon. For here was an army barely changed by modifications of warfare in India and America, an army which even disdained training in hand-to-hand combat. Surely this was not the military force to liberate Europe?

Yet some worried English politicians and visionary generals believed that Napoleon could be defeated with revisions in strategy, changes in tactics, improvements in recruiting, and in the mass production of dependable weapons. Thus a vast transformation of an antiquated army was underway by 1795 that would eventually lead to victory in the Peninsula.

The remarkable work of the duke of Richmond, master-general of ordnance (1782-83, 1784,95), for example, was instrumental in reforming artillery and engineering regiments, in securing better gunpowder, and in standardizing the manufacture of muskets in large quantities. In particular, Richmond's promotion of experimental weapons encouraged Major Henry Shrapnell of the Royal Artillery to develop in 1803 an improved case shot, effective at 400 yards, which exploded several fuses in flight over enemy columns.

Although the duke of York, the commander-in-chief (1795-1809), was unable to improve the hellrakish cavalry, his attempts to alleviate the condition of the common foot soldier earned him the sobriquet of "the Soldiers' Friend." The enlisted man, hounded from dawn to dusk, reminded often of his inferior status, fed and housed like a pauper, heretofore had lived a pitiful existence as his spirit was crushed by low wages, senseless drill, and barbaric discipline. But under York, the enlistment bounty was raised, bread was provided free to the troops, and the daily wage, unchanged since

1660, was increased to one shilling. York labored to improve food and barracks conditions, to reform courts-martial procedures, and to curtail cruel punishments inflicted upon enlisted men (1,500 lashes to one offender was the record) by limiting the flogging to a supposedly more humane 360 lashes.

In training and tactics Sir John Moore, Britains' outstanding soldier, was responsible for stressing physical fitness, improving morale, and experimenting with the Baker rifle for the Light Infantry. Instead of treating troops with the typical "scum of the earth" attitude, Moore viewed them as human beings. At Shorncliffe Camp where he trained the famed 43rd, 52nd, and 95th Regiments, Moore asserted that it was "evident that . . . discipline is carried out without severity . . . the officers are attached to the men; the men to the officers."

The standard weapon of the infantry musketeer was the familiar "Brown Bess" (East India pattern) barely changed since the 1720's. With this smooth-bore, flint-locked, muzzle-loading firearm a trained linesman could fire a round, leaden ball of ten ounces weight at the rate of three to four discharges per minute; he could utilize this primitive weapon with effect at over 200 yards, with accuracy at 100 yards, and with certainty at 80 yards. Under Moore's leadership, the newly reformed infantry regiments could fire repeated volleys with devastating effect, with speed and precision to match the French.

The perfection of the line for battle was completed by Sir Arthur Wellesley, the proud scion of Anglo-Irish ancestry who would mold the British army into a formidable instrument for victory. Entering the army in 1787, Wellesley by influence and purchase of commissions became in six years a lieutenant-colonel. He saw action in 1794-96 in the Lowlands and Baltic campaigns. It was in India, however, where he served from

1798 to 1805 that he won military distinction and where he fashioned his ideas about supplying men on the march. After a short term in the British Parliament and a minor battle in the Danish campaign (1807) to his credit, Wellesley was by 1808 a lieutenant-general and was outranked by over 200 other generals.

Wellesley was skeptical about the myth of Napoleonic military superiority. He was certain that with novel tactics, adequate use of natural cover, protection on the flanks by cavalry and artillery, his redcoats could repel the French. Sir Arthur added skirmishers to his regiments, deployed them in front of the lines, and had them concealed in depressions and behind elevations in the terrain. These sharpshooters were to pick off the French light infantry and to fire withering blasts at the advancing French column. The most significant change occurred in the deployment of the line. In order to increase the mobility and the firepower of the ranks (for often the third line of the ranks could not fire), Wellesley formed the traditional three-deep line into lines two deep.

Sir Arthur's basic strategy was based upon his observations that French forces had to disperse in order to supply themselves and that they concentrated only briefly for major battles. By avoiding a massive clash with larger French armies, by maneuvering delicately, by planning precisely to feed his men and mounts, and by encouraging guerrilla activity Wellesley believed that in prolonged campaigning he could wear down the French military machine.

If the British could establish a foothold on the Peninsula coast, he informed the Portland Ministry, Napoleon's timetable would be delayed. "It is certain," Sir Arthur asserted, "that any measure which can distress the French in Spain must oblige them to delay . . . their schemes of conquest." Convinced by Wellesley, Viscount Castlereagh, secretary of war and colonies,

The Capitulation of Madrid

ordered him to command an expeditionary force of 27,000 "for the final absolute evacuation of the Peninsula by the troops of France."

Wellesley departed from Cork in late July with 9,000 men. Another 3,000 troops left the Madeiras, 5,000 men disembarked from Gibraltar, and from the Swedish coast Sir John Moore sailed with 10,000 soldiers to join this great adventure. The French were then quelling the last Portuguese resistance and held the beaches near Oporto, the port of Peniche, and the Tagus estuary of Lisbon.

Finding no provisional junta along the Bay of Biscay willing to permit a British troop landing, Wellesley disembarked his men about 100 miles north of Lisbon on August 1 at Mondego Bay. Reinforced by troops from Gibraltar and by Portuguese units on August 10, he marched south along the coast to maintain contact with the Royal Navy. To his dismay, he was informed that he was no longer the supreme commander, nor was Moore, but that two older warriors, Sir Hew Dalrymple and Sir Harry Burrard, were his immediate superiors.

The first serious clash with the French in Portugal occurred on August 15 on the Lisbon road at Obidos from which General Alexander De Laborde and his small force skillfully retired to the village of Rolica. Here Wellesley with a larger command forced the French to retreat after a brief battle. By August 20, Wellesley had 17,000 effectives as Junot confronted him with 13,000 seasoned veterans. Junot assumed that Wellesley had strung out his regiments to the coast, and overconfident because of faulty reconnaissance about throwing the enemy into the sea, he launched six uncoordinated attacks at the British concentration in the hamlet of Vimiero. But Wellesley's rifles, concealed behind hillcrests and rock walls, blasted the French columns and his double line obliterated the surprised enemy with withering volleys every 15 seconds. The astounded Junot retreated and left clear the road to Lisbon. "We gave the French an unmerciful beating yesterday," wrote Sir Arthur in glee over the success of his tactics.

When Dalrymple arrived at Vimiero, Wellesley urged him to pursue the demoralized French, but the cautious commander hesitated to move without adequate cavalry and without Moore's infantry. Furious at such timidity, Wellesley complained that Dalrymple "prevented me from marching in pursuit of the enemy, by which he saved them from destruction." But Junot was cut off from Spain, harassed by Portuguese irregulars, and was outnumbered by a growing Allied force as Moore's army landed; hence, he requested an armistice. By the terms of the Convention of Cintra, the French retained their arms, loot, and baggage and agreed to evacuate Portugal completely in return for repatriation on British ships to France.

When the terms of the agreement were announced in England there was a great outcry of shame and disgust. The *Times* complained that "the honor of the country has been sacrificed, its fairest hopes blasted, the reputation of its arms tarnished. . . ." In the House of Commons, a caustic critic of the armistice, General Banastre Tarleton, thundered: "God forbid that we should look upon it (Cintra) in any view than as most disgraceful."

The public fury over the degree of leniency offered the French caused such an uproar that Dalrymple, Burrard, and Wellesley were recalled to explain their conduct before a military Court of Inquiry. Wellesley assumed that his army career would be terminated as he wrote his brother that "I don't know whether I am to be hanged, drawn and quartered; or roasted alive." Regardless of the intense debate about the armistice, the court voted in late December to accept the surrender terms and exonerated the three generals. As the earl of Liverpool, the home secretary, noted, Wellesley's vic-

The Siege of Saragossa

tories at Rolica and Vimiero had established the British army on the Peninsula, and "we have not lost the confidence of the Spanish people."

The Spanish were still resisting the French invasion in Zaragoza; the valiant Jose de Palafox led his heroic Aragones through another siege as 35,000 French troops surrounded the city and 150 guns pounded the crumbling walls. The Catalans of Gerona withstood repeated French assaults in a brutal struggle that lasted until December, 1809, in which the French lost 20,000 troops.

In the meantime a new form of warfare, hit and run attacks by guerrilla bands, plagued the invaders. In Castile the fiery partisan leader, *El Empecinado*, captured an entire French convoy. In Burgos, Jeronimo Merino, a daring cleric, led his men at isolated French outposts, and in Navarre, Don Francisco Espoz y Mina swooped down from the mountains to harass the conquerors. It was such fierce determination of the Spanish that tempted Sir John Moore, the commander in Lisbon since October, to take the greatest gamble of his life.

Because of Wellesley's victories and the Spanish resistance, the British Ministry had an exaggerated trust in the military capabilities of its allies and hence London supported Moore's daring scheme to cut the French supply line in northern Spain. Sir John proposed to march 400 miles through the nearly impassable north Portuguese highlands, to assist some 80,000 Spanish troops scattered all over a 200 mile front, and to concentrate his own 34,000 men at Salamanca or Burgos. Even without adequate maps, information about terrain, or even intelligence about the disposition of French or Spanish forces, the legendary Moore prepared a daring thrust into unknown territory to trap the enemy.

As he marched through Portugal in October with

17,000 troops, Moore worried over the chronic shortage of supply and transport, the lack of Allied cooperation, the torrential rains that impeded the passage of ox-carts, and the fearsome natural obstacles that confronted his dedicated army. Misinformed about the condition of roads from Portugal into Spain, Moore sent his guns and cavalry under Sir John Hope by a devious route to central Spain along the Tagus River and then north to Salamanca.

This separate expedition added two weeks and 120 miles to an already risky venture. To complicate Moore's planning for an eventual concentration of his regiments, reinforcements of 17,000 troops under Sir David Baird were delayed in disembarking and marching from the Galician port of La Coruna, and thus Baird would be tardy in joining Moore. Hence, by early November, as Moore approached Salamanca, Hope to the south and Baird to the northwest were both 100 miles away.

In the meantime unknown to Moore, Napoleon, enraged over reversals in the Peninsula, reinforced his 70,000 troops on the Ebro with 300,000 veterans led by his finest marshals of France. As his men marched over the Pyrenees, Napoleon proclaimed: "Soldiers, I have need of you. The hideous presence of the (British) leopard contaminates the Peninsula. In terror he must flee before you." Anxious to recover lost prestige over the "Spanish Affair," as he termed it, Napoleon stormed into Victoria on November 7 to direct the conquest himself.

The surprised Spanish generals, still dreaming of another Bailen, were routed within two months. The hapless Blake was beaten thrice, the count of Beledere lost at Gamonal in October, and the Spanish center under Castanos collapsed in late November at Tudela. As Burgos and Valladolid fell to the triumphant French, the entire Spanish army disintegrated. Forcing

Napoleon at rest in Spain

his Imperial Guard through the Pass of Somosierra on November 30, Napoleon marched with ease to Madrid which surrendered on December 4 to the emperor. Assuming that Moore had fled to the coast, Napoleon prepared for the final pacification of the Peninsula.

As Bonaparte was issuing decrees in Madrid, Hope joined Moore at Salamanca where the British were only vaguely aware of the Spanish disasters. Assuming that only 100,000 French troops were in Spain and that Madrid would resist like Zaragoza, Moore was still tempted to cut French lines from the Pyrenees. Aware of the danger Moore wrote that he "was risking infinitely too much, but something must be risked for the honor of the Service, and . . . to show that we stuck to the Spaniards." If Madrid toppled and the French armies turned on him, Moore realized that "we shall have a run for it."

As his entire army converged at Mayorga, north of Salamanca by December 19, Moore pondered the necessity of a quick retreat, for he now knew of Napoleon's whirlwind victories. But captured dispatches revealed that Marshal Nicolas Soult, with only 15,000 troops, was 100 miles away and that Soult was evidently unaware of the British force. Thus Soult's isolated corps at Saldana on the Carrion River was a tempting target for Moore.

Before Napoleon could snare him, Sir John Moore decided to attack Soult's force and to retire to the coast. "The movement I am making," Moore admitted, "is of the most dangerous kind." But on December 20 British patrols clashed with French cavalry, and Soult dispatched couriers with the news of the impudent Moore to Napoleon. On Christmas Eve, aware that some 200,000 French troops were advancing on his command, Moore ordered a quick retreat of 250 miles to La Coruna. He realized that Ney, Junot, Soult, and the great Napoleon himself, forging his Imperial Guard through a blizzard in the Sierra de Guadarrama mountains, were hurrying to trap him.

In a nightmarish march through winter storms Moore evacuated his discouraged army over the Esla River, blew up its bridges, and pressed on to Astorga in Leon. With some French units only 36 hours behind, Moore pushed his starving and exhausted men on a harrowing retreat unparalleled in the Peninsular War. Napoleon, finding no glory in pursuing the elusive Moore, left the chase to his marshals and departed for Paris to deal with the Austrians.

As the British retreated, they pillaged numerous Spanish towns for bread and wine. Regimental morale collapsed under the stress of constant marching through bleak terrain, the prevalence of disease in the ranks, and the constant pressure of the French on their trail. After a horrifying journey on which bodies of men and horses, guns and baggage were strewn all over the route to safety, Moore's army staggered out of the cold highland onto the warm coastal plain by January 10, 1809, to the temporary haven of La Coruna. Here supply and hospital ships awaited to rescue them from Soult's advancing horde.

With their backs to the sea as the French bombarded the town and unable to evacuate because high winds delayed the transport ships, the British made a last ditch resistance. Hiding behind village walls and barricading streets and houses, the infantry fought like devils in revenge for weeks of hell inflicted by the French. Unable to crack the British defenses and appalled at his heavy casualties, Soult withdrew. Mourning the loss of their heroic Moore who died in the battle of La Coruna, the English sailed away swearing they would return to defeat Napoleon.

Over 8,000 British soldiers were lost on this expedition to Spain, a campaign that would be debated in officers' clubs for decades on the merits of Moore's deci-

sion to advance with such daring and to retreat with
such haste. The ejection of an English army from Spain
was a bitter blow, for now the French could advance
on Lisbon from Madrid or from La Coruna. Yet there
was no Jena or Austerlitz in Galicia, for Napoleon's
marshals were tied down in the inhospitable north
provinces. Without this valiant British effort in the
winter of 1808-1809, Napoleon might have overrun the
Peninsula, and the Spanish will to resist might have
collapsed.

But as the last Asturian and Galician seaports fell,
the French juggernaut continued. In Aragon, Catalonia,
Castile, and La Mancha, Napoleon's marshals smashed
the Spanish armies. By March, 1809, the War of Independence seemed nearly over as the conquerors prepared to march on to Lisbon and Seville to obliterate
virtually the last remnants of Iberian defiance.

In London Sir Arthur Wellesley had convinced a
hesitant Ministry to entrust him with another expedition to the Peninsula. As Wellesley mobilized his troops
for the departure to Lisbon, his gallant officers, eager
for the glory and honor awarded the brave, drank regimental toasts to "a long and bloody war." Ahead of
them were five years of campaigning and the battlefield carnage of Bussaco, Talavera, and Salamanca.

After the battered British army under Sir John
Moore evacuated Spain in January, 1809, the triumphant French marshals were determined to conquer
Portugal and to eject the small Allied force at Lisbon
from its precarious foothold in Napoleonic Europe. For
this objective, Bonaparte had two armies in readiness.
To the north, at Oporto, Portugal, was Marshal Nicholas Soult's force mobilizing for a seacoast descent to the
Tagus estuary. In central Spain was another army
under Marshall Claude Victor, poised for an invasion of
central Portugal. If the puny British army could be
thrown into the sea as Moore's army had been at La

Coruna, Napoleon pontificated, the last flames of Spanish and Portuguese resistance to his imperial conquest would be extinguished.

But the dauntless Sir Arthur Wellesley arrived in Lisbon by April and defiantly shook his fist at the Napoleonic colossus. He was just as determined to retain Portugal, to invade Spain, and with resurging Iberian assistance, to throw Bonaparte's marshals back to the Pyrenees. "As long as we remain in a state of activity in Portugal," he asserted, "the contest must continue in Spain."

The more territory occupied by the 300,000 French soldiers in the vast and hostile Peninsula, Wellesley reasoned, the more difficult would be the enemy task of overwhelming his 20,000 Anglo-Portuguese troops "without exposing their whole fabric in Spain to great risk." With the minor tactical successes of Rolica and Vimiero to his credit, Wellesley hoped to achieve strategic victories by waging a campaign of precise and constant maneuvering against the widely dispersed French corps. With a liberated Portugal as a sanctuary, he believed, the British could assist their Spanish allies to recover Madrid and could cut the opponent's supply line at Burgos.

The first step in Wellesley's strategy for 1809 was to confront Soult at Oporto. Leaving 6,000 men to watch Victor, Wellesley marched north to challenge Soult on the Duero River. The British arrived on the south bank by May 12 and found the French protected by the wide Duero and ensconced in the Portuguese town. Although Soult had destroyed all connecting bridges to Oporto and had seized all river boats, his search parties had neglected four wine barges on the south bank. In addition, the marshal left unguarded a vacant convent in Oporto near the water's edge.

Wellesley would be hailed as the epitome of English prudence by future generations of conservatives. Yet on that day on the sunny banks of the Duero, he demonstrated a gambler's impulsiveness, for he dispatched 600 men to cross on the river barges in order to seize the convent. Then Sir Arthur quickly trained his artillery on the approaches to the building to protect his riflemen. Suddenly, scores of Portuguese civilians emerged from hiding with dozens of river craft to transport the entire Allied army into Oporto. Surprised by the daring of Wellesley and by the flow of redcoats, Soult evacuated the town and fled north to Galicia in a panic. At Oporto, Wellesley had another victory, and he had expelled the French completely from Portugal.

Sir Arthur next led his troops south to join the ramshackle Spanish forces in central Spain and to oppose Victor's corps strung out along the Tagus River. Unable to feed his hungry men in the bleak Extremadura, Victor was slowly retiring to Madrid. Knowing that other French armies were immersed in subjugating Spanish provinces and anticipating adequate provisions from the Spanish General de la Cuesta, Wellesley drove his tired men through the July heat over the dusty plains to snare the outnumbered Victor.

But Soult, anxious to avenge his humiliation at Oporto, hurried from Leon to aid Victor; General Sebastiani with another French army marched from La Mancha to Extremadura; and from Madrid, King Joseph and Marshal Jean Baptiste Jourdan rushed to reinforce their fellow marshal. Cuesta overslept one crucial morning while Wellesley was closing the trap and let the wily Victor recover the Madrid road. Ignoring British warnings, Cuesta impetuously pursued Victor's troops; within hours, Cuesta found himself nearly encircled by the newly arrived armies of Joseph, Jourdan, and Sebastiani.

Terrified over his predicament, Cuesta raced for the fortified village of Talavera. Cursing his Spanish allies for their blunders and for not supplying his famished troops, Wellesley had to make a stand at Talavera. In open country in any direction beyond the town, the crack French cavalry could easily cut down his infantry regiments. Surrounded by orchards and olive groves, Talavera's main defense was a hill, the Cerro de Medellin. From this strategic position through the village to the Tagus banks, Wellesley deployed his men for one of the most decisive battles of the Peninsular War.

In the sweltering heat of July 27, Victor attacked the key hill, but he failed to coordinate his assault with Jourdan and Sebastiani and was repulsed with heavy losses. Two more charges by the veteran French battalions on the village were broken by the stubborn British infantry who fired with deadly and mechanical precision at the waves of blue uniforms. In despair over the slaughter of his troops, Joseph ordered a withdrawal from the bloody engagement. "Our loss had been very great," Wellesley admitted, "that of the enemy greater . . . but we maintained all our positions and gave the enemy a terrible beating."

Unable to advance onto Madrid and fearful that his communications to Portugal would be cut by Soult, Wellesley marched his mauled legions back along the Tagus and then south to the safety of the Guadiana Valley. He was the victor in this grim contest in which for the first time in a major encounter the superiority of a steady British line against a surging French column was demonstrated. Wellesley earned the title of Lord Wellington for his exploits in the Extremadura, but more important his efforts had rekindled the fires of Spanish resistance.

One unfortunate result of his 1809 campaign was to increase Wellington's instinctive hostility to Spanish officers and to augment his disgust with their troops. Reminiscing on his narrow victory at Talavera, Wellington wrote that "the fault I committed consisted in trusting all to the Spaniards who I have since found were en-

The Siege of Tarragone

tirely unworthy of confidence." Furious at the Spanish for luring on his imperiled army with exaggerated promises of mythical food supplies and enraged over the errors of Cuesta's staff, Wellington became almost neurotic in his incessant criticism of England's ally.

"The Spanish troops will not fight, they are undisciplined, they have no officers, no provisions . . . no means of any description," he complained. "The Spaniard," claimed this paragon of English aristocratic virtues, "is an undisciplined savage who obeys no law, despises all authority . . . and is always ready with his knife and firelock to commit murder. . . ."

It was this vitriolic opinion of the hard-pressed Spanish forces and the need to repair the damage to his tattered command that caused Wellington to refuse further cooperation with the Spanish in 1809 and even to reject pleas by the British government to renew his campaign. Not until the spring of 1810, after winter cantonment in Portugal, did Wellington take to the field.

As he probed for an opening on the Portuguese border, it was apparent that the French were winning the Peninsular War in Spain. After decisive victories in 1809 over the Spanish near Toledo, Salamanca, and Aranjuez, Napoleon's troops were sweeping through the provinces. Only the cities of Murcia near and Valencia on the Mediterranean coast, Cadiz and Seville in Andalucia, and a few guerrilla strongholds still eluded the conquerors. The Supreme Junta in Seville, representing the last vestige of political authority for the imprisoned Ferdinand, was preparing to flee Cadiz. Virtually the only substantial military force still operating in the field against the French was Wellington's puny force.

While Murcia and Andalucia were being pacified, the emporor entrusted the task of obliterating the British army in Portugal to the great hero of Friedland,

Marshal Andre Massena. For seven months Massena and Wellington would spar in a strange contest for the hegemony of Portugal, a phase of the war referred to by the English general as his "cautious system."

Massena's force of 75,000 men advanced relentlessly through Leon to Portugal during the summer of 1810. By September, Massena crossed the Portuguese border and forced back the Allied army along the Mondego River to the coast. Massena aimed at Coimbra where he planned to pause for his final thrust at Lisbon.

But the tortuous route to Coimbra impeded his advance. "It is impossible to find roads worse than these," he lamented, for "they bristle with rocks; we are in a desert." Harassed by Portuguese guerrillas who conducted a "scorched earth" policy of destroying foodstuffs, livestock, and habitations, Massena nevertheless expected to occupy Coimbra by October and to terminate the campaign in Lisbon by November.

However, the Serra de Bussaco, a ridge nine miles in length, over which ran the route to the coast, delayed his advance. Here was a superb natural defense which provided excellent concealment for Wellington's infantry and artillery. He was confident that "if Massena attacks me here, I shall beat him." Just as certain was Colonel Alexander Wallace of the 88th Regiment who ordered his riflemen to "pay attention to what I have so often told you, and when I bring you face to face with those French rascals, drive them down the hill."

In five fierce assaults up the steep slopes of Bussaco on September 27, the French, seemingly forgetful of Talavera, repeatedly stormed the heights of Bussaco only to be driven back in a carnage that cost Massena 4,500 men. Wellington intended only to delay Massena, who soon found a cart road around Bussaco, but again the English general had taught the French another bloody lesson in tactics.

Protected by his cavalry, Wellington retired seventy miles to Lisbon as the French seized Coimbra. The

British barely secured their last stragglers within the defenses of Lisbon, when Massena's mighty host loomed over the horizon. Now the British redcoats and their Portuguese allies waited as Massena prepared to end the Peninsular War in Portugal by hurling them into the sea.

But the French were stunned by the obstacles that now confronted them. For the past year, under Wellington's supervision, the Portuguese had labored to protect their capital from attack by constructing a maze of interlocking defenses—the Lines of Torres Vedras. The lines consisted of three fortified zones, the outer perimeter of which stretched 30 miles from the Atlantic to the Tagus River. The entire countryside near Lisbon had been denuded of cover, stripped of trees, and razed of all protective sites.

Massena was blocked by a series of insurmountable natural and artificial obstacles—steep parapets, flooded fields, wide moats, concealed trenches, masonry walls, stone redoubts, and formidable fortresses with 430 pieces of artillery through which it was impossible for French infantry, without ponderous siege equipment, to penetrate.

Supplied from the sea and well stocked with provisions, the Allies could comfortably wait out the winter. With British gunboats controlling the Tagus estuary and with the knowledge that reinforcements for Massena had been diverted to Andalucia, Wellington was sure that he had lured Massena into a trap. Here at the impregnable position at Torres Vedras, over 300 miles from Spain, the Anglo-Portuguese force could starve out the besiegers.

The French had the choice of waiting near Lisbon or retiring to Spain. Stricken by food shortages, sickness in the ranks, and guerrilla attacks on his outposts, Massena withdrew most of his army in November to winter quarters at nearby Santarem. In December, Wellington commented that "I have determined to persevere in my cautious system . . . and to force them out of Portugal by the distress they will suffer and do them all the mischief I can upon their retreat."

By February, 1811, Massena still had not attacked. His army was starving, and without fighting a battle near the Tagus he had lost another 10,000 men. The baffled marshal ordered a mass retreat in March from the Lines of Torres Vedras to the safety of Spain. Pursued by the merciless British and the avenging Portuguese, the defeated French army of walking skeletons disintegrated on the trail back through ravaged country. Massena lost one half of his original army on this futile expedition into Portugal.

Wellington's "cautious system" represented a turning point in the Peninsular War, for the French in force would not again penetrate Portugal. With Portugal as a permanent haven, the British could prepare to take the offensive in Spain. What had been a mere beachhead on the Continent would now become the Peninsular Front which Wellington would extend over the Pyrenees to France itself.

Yet in 1811, while thwarted in Portugal, Napoleon's marshals were still masters of Spain and held the strategic fortress towns near the Portuguese border—Ciudad Rodrigo in the north and Badajoz in the south. These citadels dominated the routes into Spain, and until the Allies captured them Wellington would be unable to maintain his army on the plains of central Spain. Wellington's strategy was thus to elude repeated efforts by Massena and Soult to catch him and to press continually for an opportunity to seize one of these bastions.

Throughout the spring and summer of 1811, the opposing armies danced a grim military minuet of advance, retreat, feint, and withdraw as Wellington tried desperately to gain the few weeks needed to bombard these cities. Although Wellington inflicted a sharp defeat to Massena at Fuentes de Onoro in April, and although the English general, William Carr Beresford, with Spanish help, narrowly won a brutal battle at Albuera in May, neither citadel toppled to the Allies.

Wellington was still heavily outnumbered whenever two French corps converged on him; he lacked siege cannon, adequate digging tools, and sufficient engineers for the arduous task of investing French held citadels which seemed impervious to his brief assaults. Anguished over the mounting toll of casualties, Wellington despaired of the attempts and raised the sieges. More than mere bayonets, raw courage, and Portuguese cannon of 17th century vintage were needed to storm these sturdy fortresses.

Napoleon, far off in Paris directing the Peninsular War, inadvertantly aided the Allied cause. Disregarding the protests of Soult and Marmont, Napoleon transferred 30,000 troops from the Portuguese border to assist in the containment of new insurrections in Catalonia, Valencia, and Andalucia. In addition, the emperor drained off seasoned battalions from every corps in Spain for service in his proposed invasion of Russia. The French, under these circumstances, could no longer maintain the initiative on the Portuguese border; most of the future pattern of maneuvering in northern Spain would be determined by Wellington.

In preparation for his offensive in 1812, Wellington had perfected the organization of his army for sustained operations in the field. He had ended the cumbersome system known as Councils of War (traditionally called to plot a campaign) and developed instead the concept of a permament staff of nine units (ordnance, engineers, paymaster, commissariat, quartermaster-general, adjutant-general, surgeon-general, military secretary, military security), an institutional structure that would emerge by World War I as a general staff.

Wellington had only four full infantry divisions in 1809; by 1812, his army, steadily reinforced by an England dedicated to defeating the Corsican tyrant, expanded to eight infantry and two cavalry divisions. Each infantry division had its own field brigade of artillery (six guns), its mule and oxen train, ambulance corps, and engineers, and theoretically it could function independently on a campaign.

Wellington labored to improve the army's intelligence units by a variety of methods. He demanded detailed maps of the Peninsula; by 1810 the entire terrain of Portugal had been mapped, and by 1812 army cartographers provided his staff with revised maps of northern Spain. He improved the postal service, the message center, and the system of semaphore signaling among divisions.

Wellington relied heavily for data about the enemy from partisan scouts and from friendly peasants, but the best source of information, Wellington claimed, was the village priest, whose influence "was enormous in Spain." Wellington boasted that "there was never so perfect a system of espionage as the one . . . in Spain; all the cures were in (my) interest, and the French never did or said a single thing that (I) did not know."

The most significant administrative reform under Wellington, however, was his attention to provisioning marching troops with a modernized commissary service. In contrast to Napoleon who once blurted that "A man such as I does not take much heed of the lives of a million men," Wellington demonstrated intense concern for the rank and file during the Peninsular War.

In the 18th century, European armies sustained themselves during their March-to-October maneuvers by depending mainly upon supply depots for harvest provisions and, in an emergency, upon their success in foraging and plundering. However, since the 1790's the French, stressing speed and mobility, abandoned the

The Siege of Valencia, January 9, 1812

orthodoxy of supply depots, traveled with relatively few supplies, and relied instead on widespread foraging and forced requisitions from conquered populations.

Wellington reverted to the traditional depot system, kept the commissary with its mules and ox-carts abreast of his troops, and in order to maintain the support of Iberian peasants he insisted upon prompt payment to them for foodstuffs. Moreover, the British fought in relatively bleak areas where cities and markets were far apart, and where agriculture, traditionally low in productivity, was repeatedly devastated by marauding armies. To overcome these environmental difficulties, Wellington established nearly 40 depots to supply his men with food on their marches into Spain.

Wellington calculated the daily food requirements of his men (one pound of meat, one pound of bread or biscuit, and one pint of wine per man) and his animals (large quantities of oats, hay, and cut straw). He figured that, given a three to five day ration in their 60-70 pound packs and supplied by a supporting commissary, his men could travel 15 to 20 miles daily in a test of mobility and of endurance that would surpass even the French.

Wellington handled his troops with care, for Peninsular veterans, he asserted, were worth two recruits and were too valuable to lose to hunger and disease. Wellington, although never treated with the adoration that the typical French soldier bestowed on Napoleon, and regardless of his harsh disciplinary role and his brusque mannerisms ("I have no small talk," he admitted), pondered constantly about the condition of his troops.

The days of "spit and polish"—spotless uniforms, pipe-clayed belts, white breeches, long gaiters, clumsy headgear—were now symbolic of another era, for Wellington, careless about his own attire, was relatively indifferent about uniform regulations. In this reformed and professionalized British army, kept in readiness to strike into Spain, Wellington's major concerns were that his men be fed and be ready to fight.

In the old regime, usually only 200 days were considered suitable for military operations because of inclement weather and food shortages for men and mounts. But the French marshals, inspired by Napoleon's example, marched in any weather and bivouacked in any terrain; consequently, the attrition rate of troops was appalling. Wellington, more conscious of the value of expensive soldiers, disliked to bivouac in cold weather (tents were unavailable until 1813) and each autumn he retired to winter quarters. But in the January cold of 1813, now supplied with adequate ox-carts, siege equipment, and engineering personnel, Wellington, supposedly the military traditionalist, surprised his adversaries by striking on the Agueda River at Ciudad Rodrigo.

The unsuspecting French corps confronting the Anglo-Portuguese army were strung out from Toledo to Salamanca. After hauling ponderous cannon by bullocks through the mired route to Cuidad Rodrigo by January 7, the British sappers and engineers toiled in sleet and snow to dig the intricate system of tunnels, trenches, and embankments necessary to position the heavy artillery.

For ten days the British batteries bombarded the medieval walls of the French bastions. By January 19, with Marmont only 50 miles away from the siege, the outer redoubts fell and two breaches were made in the city's fortifications. A furious infantry assault in the face of belching French cannon broke the resistance, and the bastion toppled to Wellington.

After garrisoning Ciudad Rodrigo to ward off Marmont, Wellington next astounded the French by appearing on March 16 in the Guadiana Valley at the gates of Badajoz. This citadel was well fortified, amply

provisioned and had high, thick walls. The British estimated that Soult's army, hurrying from Seville to relieve the siege, would appear within three weeks.
Heretofore cautious about risking lives in battle, Wellington deliberately ordered wave after wave of assault
teams to storm the defiant fortress.

Three breaches by his heavy guns were made by
April 6, but after more pounding and still another desperate rush at the massive masonry, the attackers were
again repulsed. Just as Wellington was about to quit in
disgust, troops of the Fifth Division made a daring
escalade by ladders up a castle wall and entered the
city to open the gates for their triumphant comrades.
"The assault was bloody business," admitted Wellington who wept as he read the casualty list of men lost at
Badajoz.

With control of these vital gateways and with sufficient cavalry to conceal his movements, Wellington
now had the opportunity to penetrate boldly into Spain
against Marmont. Through June and July the Allied
army marched further and further along the Duero
River into Old Castile. Marmont and Wellington, each
commanding 50,000 men, both probed for openings as
they skillfully maneuvered for some advantage. At the
hills of Los Arapiles near Salamanca, on a torrid July
22, Wellington faked a hasty retreat.

Marmont assumed that Wellington, victorious thus
far only in defensive actions, would not risk an attack.
The French left wing, anxious to outflank the British
right, separated itself from Marmont's center and created a wide gap in the advancing columns. Quickly, Wellington ordered a mass attack through the opening. Superb staff work by his hardened generals, climaxed by
an overpowering cavalry charge led by General Sir Sta-
pleton Cotton, gave Wellington another victory. "By
God, Cotton," exclaimed Wellington in delight, "I
never saw anything so beautiful in my life."

The triumph at Salamanca was a monumental battle in the Peninsular War. The demoralized French marshals realized with awe that the British line on the offensive had obliterated one quarter of Marmont's army within one hour. "There was no mistake; everything went as it ought," wrote Wellington in his dispatches, "and there was never an army so beaten in so short a time."

Shocked at the defeat of Marmont, King Joseph evacuated Madrid as Wellington entered Valladolid. By August 11 the British marched in triumph through the Spanish capital. "We were the first regiment to enter Madrid," noted Private William Wheeler of the 51st. "I never before witnessed such a scene," he recalled, for the inhabitants "called us their deliverers and saviours," and presented the troops with wine and flowers.

Wellington, typically uncomfortable in such a joyous spectacle, realized that Madrid could be held only briefly, for Joseph and Soult, unimpeded by fumbling Spanish generals, were regrouping their forces and were advancing onto the capital. Leaving General Rowland Hill to ward off the French from Madrid, Wellington attempted in September a siege of the great prize—Burgos.

But Wellington had insufficient guns and ammunition to pound the sturdy walls of the old Moorish castle; he had outdistanced his supply train and Hill in Madrid was in danger. "I raised the siege of Burgos and retired," Wellington explained, "not because there was any pressure upon me, but because I did not think Hill secure; and I knew that if he were obligated to retire, I should be lost."

Worried about a potential threat to either Badajoz or Ciudad Rodrigo, Wellington left Burgos in October for the Duero. Hill retreated from Madrid over the Guadarrama Mountains to join Wellington by early November at Salamanca. After ten months of grueling campaigning, even Wellington decided to retire to winter cantonments at Ciudad Rodrigo where he summarized his efforts in 1812 by noting that "I played a game which might succeed . . . and pushed it to the last . . . with a handsome retreat to the Agueda."

A less admirable military withdrawal was Napoleon's own tortuous retreat from Moscow in the bitter winter of 1812 with the decimated remnants of a once-proud army of 500,000 strong. At both ends of Europe that year, in Russia and in Spain, the deteriorating Napoleonic legions were being challenged in a mighty resurgence of nationalism. As Russia, Prussia, Sweden, and finally Austria massed huge armies for the mighty War of Liberation in Germany, the French in Spain had to relinquish Galicia and Asturias in the north and virtually all territory from Madrid and Valencia to Cadiz in the south.

Through the spring of 1813, Wellington prepared for his final offensive across Spain to the Pyrenees. Reinforced with English and Portuguese troops, and appointed commander-in-chief of the Spanish armies, he had 100,000 men in his command, a numerical superiority over the French for the first time in years.

Clinging to northern Spain, Joseph had 60,000 soldiers posted between Toro and Tordesillas on the Duero to block Wellington's anticipated thrust at the Salamanca-Valladolid road. Yet, again Wellington outfoxed his opponent by a deceptive maneuver and by a shift in the supply route. He sent General Sir Thomas Graham with 40,000 men on a wide, flanking movement through the supposedly impassable Tras Os Montes, while the rest of Wellington's force, heavily screened by cavalry, marched toward Salamanca.

As the spirited British army poured over the Duero in early June, the hapless Joseph retired first to Valladolid, then to Burgos, and finally to the Ebro River. In the meantime, in order to shorten his lengthening supply line from Lisbon and Oporto, Wellington had the Royal Navy provision his army from Bilbao and Santander on the Biscay coast. Regardless of his 300 mile march in four weeks, Wellington could thus provision his men by shorter supply routes from the sea.

The perplexed Joseph prepared to defend his position in Navarre at Vittoria. Wellington again outflanked him with a separate force that penetrated the Cantabrian Mountains to enter the upper reaches of the Ebro Valley. On June 21 the confident Allied army attacked and punched in the French center. The vanquished enemy at Vittoria left behind guns, loot, and baggage in a disastrous retreat to the Pyrenees. Except for a small French force in Catalonia, the Anglo-Portuguese-Spanish armies under Wellington's command had finally broken Bonaparte's grip on the Peninsula.

While the Allied army conducted sieges of Pamplona and of San Sebastian, the last French strongholds in northern Spain, Soult made a daring attempt in July through the passes of Maya and Roncesvalles to throw back Wellington's divisions. Wellington, however, adroitly repelled Soult at the Battle of the Pyrenees, and by early October he led his men into France.

The Peninsular War merged with the War of Liberation as Napoleon's Empire came crashing down. Although the French had trounced the Russians and Prussians in the spring of 1813, by the summer, long hesitant Austria joined the coalition against Napoleon. Even the emperor's brilliant victory at Dresden in August was not enough to stem the tide. After the brutal battle of Leipzig in October, Napoleon's armies retreated to the Rhineland while Wellington in southern France pushed Soult back to Bayonne.

During the early months of 1814 the armies of Austria, Prussia, Russia, and Sweden invaded northern France. To the south, Wellington fought a series of bitter engagements with the tenacious Soult climaxed in April by the siege of Toulouse. But Paris capitulated to England's allies on March 31, and on April 6 the great Napoleon, still reluctant to admit defeat, abdicated his throne for confinement at Elba. By an irony of history, Napoleon and Wellington, the titans of the age, would clash in the last battle of the Napoleonic Wars fifteen months later at Waterloo.

The great tragedy of the Peninsular War, with its wreckage of pillaged cities and devastated provinces, was that if there had not been such a fiery xenophobic outburst against the Napoleonic Empire, budding liberal forces in Iberia, inspired by the Enlightenment and the French Revolution, might have prodded Spain and Portugal to participate in the broad trend of 19th century liberalism under constitutional governments.

The Peninsular War was supposedly a mere "sideshow" compared to the more spectacular Napoleonic invasion of Russia and the more grandiose struggles in northern Europe during the War of Liberation. Yet the fighting in Spain and Portugal did more to undermine Napoleon's empire than any other theater of war, and the years of constant warfare constituted a period of regular military operations sustained longer than any other campaign in Europe until World War II.

If there is a lesson to be gained from this war, aside from the study of a remarkable British general and the development of guerrilla tactics, it concerns the failure of military conquerors on alien soil. The attempted subjugation of Spain and Portugal was destined to collapse because of an intrinsic cultural factor. Despite their technological preponderance and professional superiority, the French armies failed to develop an ideology that appealed to Iberian societies. Napoleonic military might was inadequate to conquer a proud, defiant people determined to maintain their dignity and their heritage against the power of the invaders.

GOYA:
THE
DISASTERS
OF WAR

A Spanish national hero and among the most profound artists in the history of painting, Francisco Goya was at the peak of his fame when Napoleon invaded his beloved Spain in 1808. In Madrid he was the anguished observer of the first scenes of bloodshed. Goya abandoned the intellectual reasoning which caused many of his friends to cling to their allegiance to France as the brutality of the French attack was more than he could tolerate. Disillusioned with politics and war, he recorded his horror in a series of etchings, "Disasters of War," in what seems a single vision of terror and passion. Four of the etchings are reproduced on the following pages, along with Goya's original captions.

There Isn't Time.

Great Prowess! With Dead men!

This Is Bad.

Unhappy mother!

Xavier Mina

HISPANIC HISTORY'S FIRST GUERRILLA FIGHTER

By William F. Lewis

*F*rancisco Xavier Mina and Ernesto "Che" Guevara were men of the same breed and were two of Hispanic history's most dynamic guerrilla fighters. Though separated by more than a century of time and thought, each was a romantic and an inspiration to many. Guevara was the architect of Fidel Castro's Cuban Revolution, which started from Mexico in 1956 and in which were utilized some of the most effective guerrilla tactics. One hundred and fifty years earlier, Mina fathered guerrilla warfare in northern Spain as he battled against the well-trained armies of Napoleon Bonaparte.

Though the political philosophies of Mina and Guevara were obviously little related, their methods of combat were very similar, and each was, first and foremost, a *guerrillero*. While Guevara graduated from medical school in Buenos Aires in 1953 to begin a career as a guerrilla, Mina, in 1808, abandoned his studies for the priesthood in Zaragoza to do the same. For both Mina and Guevara death came early at the hands of a firing squad. The life of "Che" is talked about by many; it is a story which is now being told. Mina's life, however, has remained for a century one of history's many secrets.

There were only twelve small houses in the dusty village of Otano in the year 1789. One of these belonged to Juan Jose Mina and his wife Maria Andres, who in July of that year welcomed the arrival of their first son, Martin Francisco Xavier Mina Larrea. This handsome lad was destined to add fervor and vitality to the age that produced him.

Mina was eighteen and a student at the University of Zaragoza when he learned that Napoleon's armies had invaded Spain in the year 1807. Mina's transformation from student to guerilla warrior, though sudden, was in keeping with his lusty personality. By the end of May he was fighting in the ranks of a volunteer brigade just outside Pamplona

All of Spain reacted violently to the French takeover. Spaniards loathed Joseph Bonaparte and denounced the *afrancesados* as collaborationists. A veritable peoples' war took shape rapidly, not only in northern Spain, but throughout the peninsula, a war more violent than the popular resistance Napoleon would later encounter in Russia and the Germanies. The Spanish rallied to inspire occupied Europe as they hurled a challenge to the world's most formidable dictator.

All who were physically able fought tenaciously, using pistols, knives, axes, and even stones. French sentries were ambushed in the dead of night and brutally slain. It was a dog-eat-dog war of arson, sabotage, and plunder. Ruthless resistance movements sprang up throughout Spain. Amidst the chaos, those professing a loyalty to Ferdinand VII and a return to orderly government found themselves involved in terrorism in which the French, the *afrancesados,* and even innocent Spaniards became victims.

Nonetheless, the French attempt to establish an administration failed completely, even when Napoleon himself came down to pummel Spanish armies. The patriots, too, had trouble setting up an administration since the French were in possession of all strategic centers and the Spanish king was held prisoner in France. The civilized society of Spain was near collapse as the ravages of war increased.

At that time many guerrilla bands in Spain had become notorious for their disorderly behavior. Instead of battling the French, they plundered the hapless pueblos, stealing food, livestock, and whatever else they could find. The *guerrilleros* led by Juan Esaguirre y Gil and the Brigadier Don Mariano Renovales were constantly plagued by the violent actions of headstrong volunteers who refused to obey orders.

Renovales, a Vizcaino and a man who had distinguished himself in the Spanish militia in Argentina, returned to Spain in 1808 and was made a brigadier at Zaragoza, only to be captured by the French army when his troops refused to follow orders. Though Renovales later escaped and won honors as an able military leader, he experienced the confusion and frustration of trying to command men in a guerrilla campaign. It was Xavier Mina who would organize a truly effective force in the rugged terrain of northern Spain in the province of Navarre.

By July, 1809, Mina was readying his soldiers. The nucleus of his band consisted of twelve men, all of whom had gathered in Pamplona to hear his proposal. This colorful group included a number of Mina's boyhood friends, among them Felix Sarasa, Romon Elordio, and Lucas Gorriz. The guerrilla band became known as the *Corso Terrestre de Navarra,* and as the unit grew in number so did its heroic deeds. By the end of the war, French generals in the north knew well the name Xavier Mina.

The small band entered into active guerrilla warfare on August 12,1809, when they ambushed a French supply train between Pamplona and Tafalla and succeeded in capturing ten French cannon. Later that month, after joining forces with various other bands in Monreal, all under Mina's leadership, the well-trained *corso* captured an entire French regiment, sixty mules, and a large supply of food. By that time, Mina's command had swelled to two hundred. In September, another guerrilla force under Gregorio Cruchaga joined ranks with Mina and assisted in the capture of a mail caravan running between Barasoain and Pueyo.

Success after success crowned the efforts of Mina's brigade; by October the French General Rene D'Agoult had offered a rich reward for the death or capture of its leader.

As Mina's influence gathered momentum in the north, the *junta suprema* in Seville, established in September, 1808, within the confines of the Alcazar's moorish walls, was experiencing great difficulty. The *suprema* sent numerous appeals not only throughout Spain, but to its American dominions as well, for loyalty and support. Offers of seats in the *suprema* were made to attach colonials more closely to the national cause.

Since no other legitimate authority existed, most of the royal officials in the new world recognized the *suprema.* Nevertheless, many were dubious about placing themselves under its orders. Early in 1810 the French occupied Sevilla and most of Andalusia, forcing the *suprema* to Cadiz where in September the famous *Cortes* would convene. Meanwhile, in the north, Mina's exploits were becoming more dazzling.

As darkness settled over Pamplona and noises of

summer days gave way to soft night sounds, a screaming band of Mina's men thundered through a nearby pasture, stampeding a herd of eighty-five horses. These became the nucleus of Mina's newly formed cavalry unit. Utilizing information from agents in Pamplona, Aragon, and France, Mina was able to anticipate French troop movements and, with his knowledge of the terrain and his increased mobility, to frustrate the enemy advance in many areas of Navarre. By destroying supply lines, intercepting mail dispatches, and maintaining a well-organized communication with other Spanish and English leaders, Mina not only gained a wide reputation but won both the hatred and respect of the French high command.

Mina, like Robin Hood, was an adventurer of the highest order. His military exploits, though directed against the French, were also designed to win him personal pleasure and profit and to satisfy his rebel spirit. And in the process there can be little doubt that innocent people were sometimes victims. Like the bowman of Sherwood Forest, Mina did not hesitate in robbing a rich man to help a poor one. Such was the case in November, 1809, when his *guerrilleros* occupied Tudela, a small city just north of Zaragoza.

Reports of the capture of Tudela depict Mina's men as drunken bandits who plundered and ravaged the city, stealing horses, bulls, and robbing the townspeople. While this charge is not entirely untrue, it is quite certain that the raiders' motives were not purely selfish and ruthless. For it is known that the captured horses were turned over to the Spanish military and the bulls used to augment the party's dwindling food supply. And, though some atrocities did occur, the fact remains that the French were driven out of the town and Spanish control restored.

Certainly Xavier Mina was not a saint. He was, instead, a hardy man of the soil fighting a grim war. The

185

very nature of war creates a psychology in which the thinking and actions of men are transformed. Thus it was during Spain's peninsular war. Civilized society almost collapsed as the country endured six years of seizure and theft, hatred and revenge, battle and murder. No one wore a halo, and Mina was no exception.

Following the liberation of Tudela, Mina led his forces north to Los Arcos where they paused for rest and reorganization. The growing fame of the youthful band had attracted many recruits. His roving *corso* had become an international brigade filled with soldiers of fortune from all over Europe. While at Los Arcos, Mina named the valiant Cruchaga as second in command, while placing an ex-sergeant major by the name of Calvo in command of the infantry.

Mina received little war material from the outside but supplied himself principally by capturing from the enemy. By February, 1810, he and his men had collected a large quantity of arms and munitions, much of which was distributed to new volunteers throughout the countryside. The wide distribution of arms came none too soon, for on March 27, 1810, Mina was trapped by the French in the town of Labiano. After a valiant effort to escape, he was wounded and taken prisoner. He was sent to a French prison where he remained for the next four years.

Nevertheless, the guerrilla movement was just beginning and Mina's fame, which had spread throughout Spain, gave impetus to the increasing fervor of the resistance. Mina had been the father of guerrilla warfare in the north. He had turned rowdy, undisciplined bands into polished fighting units. Thus, the guerrilla effort continued under Mina's uncle, Espoz y Mina, who took command of the *corso*. By 1814, with invaluable support of Wellington and the British, the French were on the run.

After the war and Ferdinand's restoration Mina was

released from prison (April, 1814) in exchange for the release of several leading French military figures. Upon his return to Spain, Mina could not stomach the repressive policies of Ferdinand VII. At the same time, he was angry because Ferdinand refused to offer him a high position in the Spanish army. Thus, after an abortive attempt to overthrow the crown's control in Pamplona, Mina, branded a traitor, fled to England in 1815.

At that time, London was alive with commerce and trade, both legal and illegal. Committed to an alliance with Spain, Britain was formally bound to respect Spain's position vis-a-vis her revolting colonies. Officially England adhered to a policy of neutrality while Spain struggled to hold on to her new world possessions. Nevertheless, commercial and economic pressures constantly led to violations of the neutrality by English subjects; and though the British government dubbed these activities illegal, they continued and increased.

Mina had no definite objective when he arrived in England. He had little money and no close friends. His first three months were actually spent in a small hamlet outside London. It was there that he met a wealthy Englishman whose sentiments, like his own, were of a liberal character. Mina became fast aware of the unlimited possibilities for one seeking wealth, adventure, and a just cause. Within three weeks he was offered leadership positions in a number of privateering and insurgent expeditions bound for the new world. He accepted no offers.

In May he moved to London where he met Fray Servando Teresa de Mier, a leading liberal and intellectual from Mexico, and a man destined to change the course of Mina's life. Within a month after their initial meeting, they organized an expedition to Mexico. Their plan was to lead an army of rebels under Mina to Mexico (New Spain); to move inland from Veracruz, to consolidate all the existing patriot forces under his command; and finally to march on Mexico City.

Servando undoubtedly had much to do with inducing Mina to choose New Spain as a center of operations. Being a native of Mexico and an expert on the causes of the insurrection, Mier was deeply committed to the struggle of "his people." Mina, meanwhile, had many opportunities to seek his fortune and fame in other areas. Both Simon Bolivar and Miguel Carrera sought to enlist the dashing Xavier. However, not wanting to place himself under the command of another, Mina chose to lead his own expedition.

By May, 1816, the expedition, supported by British and American capital, was ready to depart. Some two hundred men boarded the *Calendonia* on May 15 and sailed to Baltimore. There Mina and Mier recruited additional manpower and financial aid and were assisted by young Winfield Scott. From Baltimore, with three new ships, Mina sailed on to Haiti to try and enlist the support of Simon Bolivar.

On October 12, 1816, Mina arrived in Haiti and was welcomed by President Alexandre Petion and a British commercial agent named Robert Sutherland. Mina met with Bolivar in Sutherland's home the following day. He proposed that Bolivar join his expedition to Mexico. Following a victory over the Spanish there, Mina promised to return to New Granada under Bolivar's command. Bolivar was interested and for several days remained in a state of indecision. His dilemma was reflected in a letter to General Brion: "I don't know since Mina arrived whether or not I shall change my plans. I spoke with him yesterday very frankly and what he tells me makes me hesitate to go ahead with my own designs."

What would have happened had Bolivar joined the Mina expedition? This question, of course, cannot be answered. But it is indeed intriguing that Bolivar, after two crushing setbacks in Valencia, did seriously consider joining the independence cause in Mexico. His decision to go would certainly have changed the Spanish-American independence story.

Though Bolivar ultimately rejected Mina's proposal, Xavier was able to enlist the aid of Petion who provided the expedition with a division of men. Mina then sailed for Galveston where he made final preparations for the invasion. On April 18, 1817, Mina and company made a successful landing at Soto la Marina (near Tampico). The expedition was underway.

Little time was wasted in setting up a printing press from which were issued a series of proclamations made by Mina to be distributed throughout the country. He hoped to rally the people to his banner. His plan was to move inland to the best protected rebel strongholds of Peotillos, Juaxilla, and Los Remedios. In each he hoped to win the support of a large contingent of fighting men who would serve under his command against the Spanish. Then, with an estimated ten thousand men he would launch the decisive battle.

Leaving Mier in charge at Soto la Marina, Mina moved inland. Stunning victories at Valle de Mais, Real de Pinos, and Peotillos were dramatic proof that Mina was not to be taken lightly by the royalists. Within a month he had captured over seven hundred enemy troops and had moved well into enemy territory.

Mina's first major encounter at Valle de Mais was crucial. It took place on the eighth of June. Mina had halted his division in a small wooded area several miles from town. Beads of perspiration dotted the faces of both him and his second in command, Colonel Robert Young, as they listened intently to the elderly peasant woman sitting before them. She reported that the enemy, some four hundred strong, all cavalry, had taken up a position just outside of town and were, it appeared, determined to stop Mina's advance.

This announcement brought a thunderous cheer from Mina's men. After ten days of continual marching over sun-parched terrain, all were eager for action. A strong bond was fast developing between Mina and all those who had joined the expedition since its arrival in Mexico. Xavier's magnetic personality commanded respect and admiration.

The division advanced upon the village cautiously until the exact location of the enemy had been ascertained. The royalists had taken up a position three miles from the town on a high plateau which overlooked the main road. From this point they hoped to launch a surprise attack as Mina's band moved forward.

Dispatching the main body of troops along the road as a decoy, Mina led a small number of veteran warriors over the hill and through the dense underbrush. Silently, his guerrillas took up strategic positions and waited for the enemy to come into view on the road below. At the moment they appeared, Mina gave the order to attack. The royalists, thinking themselves surrounded, began a retreat.

Quickly, Mina selected fifty of his best cavalrymen, and after ordering the main body of his troops to proceed to the village, took up the chase, pursuing the fleeing royalists to a point several leagues beyond Valle de Mais. Not far from the town, a small number of soldiers rallied briefly. "However, when the general (Mina), at the head of his men, dashed in among them, they broke and fled."

Mina's men trailed the enemy two leagues further, seized one gun and a small cannon, and then returned to Valle de Mais. Though two rebel soldiers were severely wounded, only one had been killed. "Furthermore," according to Brush, "the personal intrepidy and skill displayed by the general on this occasion, produced in the minds of the division, not only devotion to him, but the most unbounded confidence in his abilities."

Mina's jubilant forces occupied the town on the evening of June 9, and were received by the populace, whose attitude was a mixture of both fear and gratitude. Mina quickly relieved their apprehension by issuing the strictest orders that none of his men engage in any act of plunder or personal violence.

Throughout the month of July, Mina continued to confound the enemy. He led a number of surprise attacks against well-fortified royalist outposts near Sombrero, all with complete success. By the end of the month posters were seen throughout the countryside: (1) Anyone who assists the rebel Mina in any manner will suffer penalty of death and confiscation of all property. (2) Anyone who captures Mina and delivers him to a royalist military commander or judge will be given 1,500 pesos and will be forever freed from royalist taxation. (3) If this person is a military man he immediately will be raised in rank. If he is a man who is now a rebel, he will receive immediate pardon for his crime and a reward of 1,500 pesos. If he is a foreign adventurer, he will receive the same amount of money and free passage to his homeland.

Within the next three months the royalists mobilized to crush Mina. The young rebel, while successful in battle, had been unable to ally with other patriot leaders, none of whom were willing to relinquish their command, particularly to a Spaniard. Thus, Mina was forced to continue alone with his small band while the enemy closed in.

On October 27, 1817, the royalist General Francisco de Orrantia with a large well trained cavalry unit led a surprise assault against Mina. Xavier led an inspired defensive effort which lasted for several hours. Outnumbered fifty to one, however, the rebels were forced to surrender and Xavier was taken prisoner.

On a foggy morning before the sun had awakened the day, Xavier Mina, twenty-eight years of age, was marched under guard from the stockade and taken to a small clearing on the green hillside above Los Remedios. Though the fort below was still under siege by other rebels, all guns were quiet. Except for the few who kept patrol, the combatants on both sides slept. Quickly and silently Mina was led up the hill to a spot designated by the royalists. The blindfold was removed from his eyes; he looked down at his wet shoes, around which the blades of grass glistened with the morning dew.

The royalist commander announced to his men the nature of Mina's crime against the crown. Before the signal was given to fire, Mina stepped forward and said only, "Take good aim, and don't make me suffer." Then the officer gave his order and a single volley broke the morning silence.

Mina's contribution to the struggle for independence was the greatest a man could give—his life. He lived a very full twenty-eight years, and while he enjoyed the rugged *guerrillero's* lot and relished the excesses of this existence, he remained dedicated to the liberal cause which had carried him to Mexico.

Yet historians, when describing the Peninsular War in Spain or the independence struggle in New Spain, pass lightly over the name Xavier Mina. Why? The answer appears to be simple: Mina failed. It was not Xavier Mina who was seen driving the French across the Pyrenees in 1814, but his uncle Espoz y Mina. And it was not he who secured Mexican independence in 1821, but a man named Iturbide.

Though Mina performed many a daring and successful military exploit against his enemies, often against overwhelming odds, he was never on hand to bask in the glory of final victory. Yet, in the writing of history one cannot, one must not, ignore the deeds of those who

Simon Bolivar

fail, for the failure of one man can be, and often is, the basis for another's success. Though Mina perished in 1817, the spirit of liberalism and dedication which he symbolized was sustained long after Mexican independence had been achieved.

Dowager Empress Tzu Hsi

MIDSUMMER MADNESS OF 1900

by Angela Stuart

*I*t was officially summer in Peking. The imperial edict had just gone out ordering the court to change from springtime silk robes without embroidery to summer robes embroidered with the lotus flower. On the surface there was no variation in the immemorial routine within the vermilion walls of the Forbidden City. But early in June of 1900, the Dowager Empress Tzu Hsi held a fateful audience in the throne room of her palace of Ming Shou. One side of the hall being almost entirely of glass, the other only partially of latticework, the effect was that of wooden columns supporting a roof between glass. Dawn was breaking and cold daylight crept into the room where colored lanterns suspended from lacquered poles glowed fitfully.

From her throne of teakwood mounted on a dais, the

Members of the secret society of Boxers

empress, wearing the imperial yellow dragon robe of state, intently watched the performance taking place in a cleared space in the center of the hall where two men in warlike regalia, armed with swords, were stabbing furiously at a short, unarmed figure stripped to the waist, who, dodging and whirling, miraculously avoided the tips of their weapons yet never veered from one spot on the floor.

Two nobles knelt on yellow cushions at either end of the dais—Tuan, a prince of the blood, and Jung Lu, grand councilor. Tuan, his face covered with smallpox scars, his eyes small and ferret-like, had scorned his own class, and against the sternest Manchu house laws had made friends with China's riffraff. Consumed with fanatical race hatred, he had spent years organizing members of the secret society of Boxers into military bands for the express purpose of destroying every foreigner and Christianized Chinese in the Middle Kingdom. He had fetched the mountebanks to perform for the empress to prove that no weapon could take the life of a Boxer. The entire success or failure of his campaign depended upon the outcome of the duel.

Furtively he watched Tzu Hsi's face, her eyes impenetrable as black enamel, her features impassive as a death mask. While the two armed men redoubled the fury of their assault, the half-naked man leaped and whirled, seeming to have eyes in the back of his head, never receiving so much as a scratch. Tzu Hsi's hands, the long nails on the third and fourth fingers protected by a golden shield flashing with rubies, jade, and pearls, opened and closed convulsively on the yellow armrests of her throne.

At last the contest was finished. The two armed warriors, exhausted, bathed in sweat, dropped to their knees before the dais and kowtowed. Their victim, fresh as when he had entered the arena, also knelt and knocked his forehead three times on the tiles.

避亂圖

同文滬報隨報附送不准及售畫辰第卅一頁六月初二圖

A Shanghai newspaper cartoon showing the flight of Europeans from the threat of the Boxers

After they had withdrawn, the empress demanded in a suppressed voice, "What would you have me do, Prince Tuan?"

Instantly he replied, "Give me leave, Your Majesty, to send my Boxers forth to slay the foreigner. Give me leave to open fire tomorrow morning upon the foreign legations."

Tzu Hsi hesitated. In her agitation her cheekbones were sharpened and the veins on her forehead protruded. Finally she raised her small right hand, palm up, then closed it until the knuckles were white. It was the consent for which Tuan had been waiting. He kowtowed rapidly, and scarcely able to conceal his exultation, backed from the throne room.

It was incumbent upon Jung Lu to follow, but he did not stir from his cushion. He had grown up with the empress in the Tartar City, one of the concentric, walled enclosures which make up Peking. Together they had caught dragon flies on the banks of the Jade Canal. Then she had been called Lan Kuei, the Orchid. As a result of his lifelong devotion, he enjoyed privileges denied to any other courtier.

Officially the audience was ended when the voice of the sovereign ceased. But Jung Lu defied protocol to protest against the chicanery they had just witnessed. He reminded the empress that it was contrary to the law of nations to attack the accredited representatives of foreign powers, that the sudden outcry "Slay the foreigner!" would provoke hostilities on all China's frontiers.

But the empress was not one to retract her word, once given. She was in her third regency. Her power was absolute and her edicts beyond question. With a single gesture she had committed the throne, as well as some six thousand Manchu princes and imperial clansmen, to the atrocities of the Boxer Uprising.

The Manchus had always followed an anti-foreign as

well as an anti-Chinese policy. Like all the conquerors of China, they had come from the north, rugged Tartar tribesmen descended from Tamerlane's invincible hordes. After overthrowing the Ming Dynasty, which was purely Chinese, they established garrisons throughout the empire, drawn from the eight Manchu banners or divisions. As the sign of their domination, they imposed the partly shaven head and queue on every man. But as a ruling class they were spread thin. In 1900, three million Manchus governed some four hundred million Chinese.

The *mystique* of their hold on China was chiefly due to their aloofness. To the native Chinese they were a sacred clan of untouchables. The strict ban against marriage between Manchus and Chinese went far toward sustaining this reputation. Manchu nobles were even forbidden to frequent native haunts of amusement under pain of death.

But by the end of the nineteenth century the sleeping dragon of China was beginning to stir. The Manchus feared the infiltration of foreign influences as likely to rouse it to the point where it would awaken and destroy everything.

The empress's own implacable hatred of the men-from-afar went back to the Arrow War of 1859 and the burning of the summer palace. It was a time when industrialized Europe had been seeking added facilities for trade. As a first step toward prying open the doors of China, the foreign powers demanded that they be allowed to send their representatives to the Dragon Throne. This the Manchus refused. For more than a century they had allowed European traders within the port of Canton the refreshment of a walk in the Fati flower gardens. But this was sufficient. It was unthinkable that barbarians should penetrate the Forbidden City, that last and innermost enclosure where everything was clandestine, veiled, and sealed.

However, pressure was brought to bear upon the dying Emperor Hsieng Feng, in 1858, to sign the Treaty of T'ientsin with Great Britain and France after agreeing to receive their ministers. The following year the treaty was broken when foreign diplomats were refused entry to the country, and the Chinese seized her majesty's ship *Lorcha Arrow*. What followed would be known as the Arrow War.

Anglo-French forces landed in T'ientsin to protest the violation of the treaty. Thirty-eight officers and interpreters were dispatched from the Allied camp to Peking to discuss the matter. But for the Manchus there was nothing to discuss. They bound the envoys with ropes and threw them in a courtyard where they were exposed to burning sun by day and intense cold by night. Water had been poured on the ropes to tighten them. The ropes cut into the flesh and gangrene set in. Many died.

When the Anglo-French army marched on Peking to avenge the torture and death of the envoys, they could find no responsible officials. The court had left hurriedly on an "Autumn Tour of Inspection."

After an encounter with Tartar cavalry in which the Manchu force was completely routed by French rifled artillery, the foreign troops came to the summer palace, some sixteen miles outside Peking on a slope of the Western Hills. Known as Yuan Ming Yuan, it was a network of verandahed pavilions filled with art treasures accumulated by seven generations of Manchus. The buildings were carved, gilded, lacquered; the walls were of shimmering silk traced with shadowy, insubstantial embroideries; the columns were entwined from top to bottom with dragons of pure gold, the furniture inlaid with jade and precious stones.

After a cursory looting, Lord Elgin, the British commander, gave the order to fire the palace, and everything was burnt to the ground. Only a small outlying part was ever reconstructed. In justification for such a drastic act of revenge, Lord Elgin said, "With Asiatic peoples, nothing convinces more than brutal strength, nothing succeeds like the *fait accompli*." In the case of the Manchus, they never forgave nor forgot Elgin's *fait accompli*.

The European powers had settled the moot point of representation in the Middle Kingdom. But as late as 1900 foreign diplomats in Peking met with indifferent treatment. Ministers on a visit to the empress were escorted through a side or back gate and received in a simple, inferior throne room, poorly furnished. During the session, when an ambassador refused to kowtow (and the English steadfastly refused), it brought repeated jerks on his trouserleg by a kneeling eunuch.

In the capital, the Tsung-li-Yamen was designated the foreign office. It was a dirty, cheerless, barren building where Chinese officials condescended to receive foreign envoys. The officials kept a list of the "barbarian" nations and some description of each. But on the whole they loathed business and were convulsed with merriment whenever some missionary in the interior was hit with a brick. Still, to the legations, the Tsung-li-Yamen, being a link of sorts with the supercilious Manchus, was better than nothing.

In the last years of the nineteenth century, the empire was carved more and more into foreign spheres of influence. These strategic positions were "leased" to foreign powers. It was a new diplomatic formula, thin as gauze over the reality of annexation.

The empress, who was known for her "strength of the pen," poured out her bitterness in a memorial: "They have made some score of treaties with China, containing at least ten thousand written characters. Is there a word in any one of them concerning reverence for parents, or the cultivation of virtue and respect for the nine canons of rightful conduct? No! Is there one word in any one of them as to the observance of ceremony, as to duty, integrity, and a proper sense of shame, the four cardinal principles of our nation? Again, no! All they speak of is material profit."

Tzu Hsi could not reconcile the teachings of the missionaries with what she had learned of the warlike tendencies of the foreign intruders. They had taken the Chinese explosive powder used for centuries to celebrate happy events and within one year had put it into a gun with which to kill people.

The Boxer Uprising was no sudden fanatical outburst. It was a well-planned crusade, the result of long-festering resentments: the burning of Yuan Ming Yuan; the circuiting of spiritual and material wares through treaty rights; and even such a seemingly trivial event as the garden party which the empress held for the ladies of Legation Quarter on the first of June, 1900. After receiving a quite lavish hospitality, many of the guests had walked off with gold and silverware as souvenirs of the Forbidden City. To the intensely emotional empress this was perhaps the last straw.

But in the matter of the attack on the legations, she made one concession to Jung Lu. He could take two thousand imperial troops and escort the residents of Legation Quarter to T'ientsin, at once, with the courteous suggestion it would be as well if they never returned.

Looking from the window of his green sedan chair as it left Ch'ien Men gate in the imperial wall, on the evening of June 14, Jung Lu saw roaring flames mounting to the sky above the Chinese quarter, where the Boxer fury had broken loose. Prince Tuan's forces had gleefully fired mission buildings, the homes of Christian Chinese, and shops displaying foreign goods with pitch-dipped torches, but the holocaust was spreading in all directions as the wind carried the flames to Chinese as well as foreign-owned shops, jeopardizing vast stores of treasures.

Two Boxer divisions took part in the uprising—the Ch'iem, who used yellow cloth to wrap their heads and for sashes, and the Kan or Red division, who used red. The streets of Peking were clogged with red and yellow as the Boxers poured into the capital from the provinces by tens of thousands.

Boldly Jung Lu's mounted *mafoos* preceded his chair down a narrow lane into which smoke and ashes had already drifted. As it was the beginning of summer, every shop on either side of the lane overflowed with fans: paper, ivory, silk, painted, embroidered, lacquered, or covered with gold leaf, until it seemed all Peking must be interested solely in the purchase of these delicate futile ornaments which would presently curl up and vanish in the oncoming conflagration.

The higher the rank of a passenger, the faster a chair traveled, but Jung Lu's outriders had great difficulty clearing a path through the congested streets. All peddlers with basket produce had vanished. In the marketplaces hundreds of Boxers, their faces painted black, rallied around bonfires. They shouted incantations until they fell swooning to the ground; then they got up, jumping, leaping, brandishing swords and spears, claiming to be possessed by gods. Some wore a kind of insignia, a small, bright red apron which had been dipped in the blood of the man who owned it.

The green sedan chair came to a halt before the gateway of the Legation Quarter. Sandbags were piled on the wall, and Marine guards from the eight nations represented in the quarter were posted at intervals. Early in June the legations, while unconvinced of any real danger, took the precaution of requesting a few extra guards from the man-of-war lying off Taku. Three hundred Marines were dispatched, and luckily reached Legation Quarters hours before the Boxer outbreak, thus raising the total defense of the legations to

841 Marines of all nations.

Due to the official appearance of Jung Lu's chair and the elegant livery of his outriders, he was allowed to enter. Native servants still loyal to their foreign masters were at work building a series of barricades along Legation Street, in the event the Boxers penetrated the outer wall. All the legation flags were at half-mast.

Jung Lu's chair stopped before the British Residence. Sir Claude MacDonald received his visitor in the middle of the compound. Shells from Prince Tuan's cannon, mounted on the wall of the Imperial City, exploded overhead, lighting for an instant the spring dusk as the two men stood facing each other.

Their attire was in sharp contrast. Jung Lu wore a dark, tightly belted robe embroidered with four-clawed dragons (the highest number of talons permitted to a bannerman), satin boots, and on his finely woven straw hat the red coral button, likewise indicative of the first rank in the kingdom. But these niceties were obviously wasted on the English minister, whose black sack coat and trousers were dusty and disheveled.

Jung Lu half knelt, swiftly touching his right hand to the ground, palm down, in the Manchu salutation. "Your Excellency," he said, "I have brought a message from Her Majesty, the Empress." Then, producing a scroll from a yellow silk handkerchief, he read in the dulcet Mandarin of the north:

"We direct the Grand Councilor, Jung Lu, to take two thousand trusted troops, and when the foreign envoys have fixed the date for leaving the city, to give them safe conduct to T'ientsin. If there should be evildoers who lie in wait to plunder, these are to be killed. Let there not be the slightest remissness. Before the envoys leave the Capital, if they have telegrams to send to their countries, provided they are not in code, the Tsung-li-Yamen is promptly to arrange the matter for them without delay. This will exhibit the great desire of the Throne to treat the people-from-afar with tenderness."

MacDonald's reply was cryptic. "You may tell your Empress we would not venture ten paces outside Legation Quarter, let alone a hundred miles through an inflamed province. Nevertheless, we thank her for this belated consideration on our behalf. Had she shown as much interest in our fate a week ago, it might have come to something."

As Jung Lu started back to his chair, the minister stood looking after the tall, limping figure. When a secretary joined him, he said, "There goes a strong man, the strongest of all the Manchus. If I were inclined to trust anyone, I would trust him."

The Boxers were a semi-religious sect, and so their fanaticism reacted powerfully upon the demon-ridden imaginations of the native Chinese. When they ran through the streets brandishing weapons and shouting "Kill! Kill! Kill!" they claimed to be acting in behalf of the tutelary gods of China, all of whom the foreigner had managed to offend in one way or another.

Engineers had sunk shafts into the bowels of the earth with no compunction for the fact they were jabbing the Fung Shou. Whenever possible, the Boxers remedied matters. Under the pretext that the earth dragon did not like the feel of hot steel on his back, they tore up the railway between Peking and Paotingfu; to appease the wind dragon they sawed off the telegraph poles.

But as the siege of the Legations dragged on into its second month of day-and-night bombardment, the empress suffered a bitter disillusionment in the uprising she had "mothered." The Boxers were proving all too vulnerable to foreign bullets. When they crossed the Jade River bridge, wave on wave in mass formation to rush the legation wall, they fell back before the expert marksmanship of the Marine guards until their corpses filled the river level. No doubt they were prodigious swordsmen, but they never got close enough to the Marines to prove it.

Prince Tuan, who had access to the Imperial treasury, offered his followers the equivalent of $200 for every dead foreigner. It was remembered by the Chinese that much bigger rewards had been paid for the heads of barbarians in the reign of Hsieng Feng, but then they were rare. The Boxers complained of these severed heads that they had to be exhibited in cages because there was no queue to hang them by.

Sometimes the attacks slackened for hours, or even days, on end. Once the legations sent out a message they would not fire on a white flag. They were promptly taken at their word. In the ensuing lull, hundreds of white flags appeared in the space beyond the legations and in all the surrounding streets and lanes.

Again, in the middle of a fierce daylight assault on the legation barricades, Li Lien Ying, the chief eunuch, came out from Tung Wha Men gate and posted a placard written in vermilion ink on the wall of the Forbidden City:

EDICT

A most important decree! The alarms and excursions, yelling, blowing of horns, firing of guns and booming of cannon now taking place in the Capital, have disturbed Her Majesty, the Empress-Dowager's sleep and caused her to be stricken with a dire headache. Therefore, the members of Prince Tuan's Celestial Tiger Corps are ordered to cease firing at once and refrain from all disorders until further notice is given. No mercy will be shown to offenders against this edict. Hear and obey!

Sullenly the Boxers bowed to the imperial injunction. Laying down their weapons, they squatted on their heels wherever they happened to be—on the tiled roofs overlooking the legations, on the city walls, in lanes and marketplaces, and commenced tossing rude dice made from knucklebones for their plundered spoils.

The empress paced the floor of her pavilion. Boxer fires had crept up and burned Ch'ien Men Tower over the imperial gateway. It was a very bad omen. The Boxers' ritual obsession with fire was "scorching the Throne to its very eyebrows." Narrow Lantern Street, East and West Lanes of Satchet Bags, Magpie Lane, Pearl Market Street, Coal Market Street, as well as famous Hatamen Street, had all been burnt to the ground. And there was no way of fighting the fires. They simply burned until there was no more fuel.

Before the attack, Prince Tuan had said, "What will a hundred puny hobgoblins more or less matter?" Now the empress reminded him caustically, "What indeed! You have burnt down half my capital and not taken one foot from these puny hobgoblins!"

Tzu Hsi was especially concerned for the ten thousand boxes of rare chrysanthemums in the imperial nursery. They included Dragon Whiskers, Snowball (of which the petals were edible when dropped in hot chicken broth), Golden Bells, and the Ink chrysanthemum, so deeply, darkly red it looked black. They were the empress's favorite flower. When it was time for disbudding, she would examine the hands of each of her ladies-in-waiting. Only those with the coolest hands were permitted to touch the delicate buds.

And now, continual smoke, cinders, and withering blasts imperiled the whole crop. Still she dared not issue a peremptory order to stop the siege of the legations altogether, for fear the Boxer mobs in their wrath would attack the throne itself. Even Prince Tuan's loyalty was dubious at best.,

Finally after countless false rumors that relief columns were on their way from T'ientsin, the besieged legations heard a formidable cannonading in the east. They were not Chinese guns. On August 12, the joint Allied armies stormed three gates of Peking—Ch'ao Yang Men, Tung Wha Men, and Ha Ta Men. The legation guards went out and joined them, the Christian converts acting as guides. The attackers mounted the ramp of the Chinese city over heaps of Boxer corpses in fierce hand-to-hand fighting.

On August 14, the American Minister Conger's electrifying report reached President McKinley: "We are safe."

On August 15 a proclamation went out from the Forbidden City, as once before, that the court was leaving on an "Autumn Tour of Inspection." This time it was headlong flight. Tzu Hsi twisted her long, luxuriant hair in a knot, cut her nails, and put on the blue cotton gown of a peasant woman. To avoid the destruction of the Forbidden City, the Chinese defended it only long enough to permit the court to escape. As the empress left by one gate, the foreign armies entered by another.

Hardships mounted as the imperial cortege, traveling in rough Peking carts, struggled over roads that were gullies worn down fifty to one hundred feet below the surrounding land. They were delayed by flood and cyclone. Shelter was to be found only in ruined temples and repulsive inns. As the empress wrote in a memorial, "I sleep on brushwood and taste gall."

Fleeing always toward *Ta Tsin,* the west, they crossed the Great Wall and traversed mountain passes where the track was nothing but sills and terraces hewn from the cliffs. Only Tzu Hsi rode in a sedan chair. Often it hung above appalling abysses where one slip on the part of her chair bearers would have meant her instant death. The government accompanied the empress, so she continued to rule, even in exile. Having no proper paper or envelopes, she would take a ball of waste cotton, and when it was spread on a table and ironed out, it became a long strip of paper. Imperial couriers carried her edicts, signed with the vermilion pencil, back to Peking from the remotest stopping-places.

But as months passed, and Tzu Hsi, penetrating deep into the interior of her realm, was feted by loyal mandarins of every "button," the flight altered and became in truth a tour of inspection. The carts were exchanged for imperial palanquins escorted by retainers and a large body of cavalry.

As the diplomatic aftermath of the Boxer Uprising, a Peace Protocol was signed by the Western Powers in 1901. They jointly levied an indemnity of 325 million dollars upon the Imperial Government of China. All the leaders of the rebellion were put to death with the exception of Prince Tuan. As a member of the Royal clan he was spared decapitation, but forever banished. All fortifications from the seacoast to T'ientsin, east of Peking, were abolished to give foreign troops easy access to the capital in the event of future disorders.

But reprisals would have been far worse except for Jung Lu. When the Allied troops broke into the imperial arsenal they found a shipment from Krupp of the newest artillery pieces, all still in their crates. As commander-in-chief, Jung Lu had kept the shipment safely locked up, only permitting his men to mount rusty, antiquated cannon. The Krupp artillery would have pulverized the barricades in Legation Street in a matter of hours.

There was no doubt Jung Lu, by staving off the massacre of the foreign representatives, had saved the dynasty, but only for a time. The Boxer outbreak brought momentous changes to the empire which in effect doomed the Manchus. After the suppression of the

Boxers, eight armies occupied Peking. Whereas formal war had never been declared against China, the foreigners acted as though they were living in a conquered country. The Chinese government lost complete control of large areas of Chinese territory, even whole provinces.

The Russians, under the pretext of putting down Boxer disorders, rushed troops into Manchuria, the cradle of the Manchus, and occupied much of three provinces. It was an encroachment on Chinese sovereignty. Although the Russians promised to withdraw in a year, there was no dislodging them. When the Russo-Japanese War broke out in 1904, it only substituted Japan for Russia in southern Manchuria.

Other losses had an even more direct bearing upon the throne. When the avenging armies broke into Peking, a great number of imperial clansmen and Manchu families of the highest rank committed mass suicide, depriving the empress of scores of trusted officials at a time when they were sorely needed. All in all, the results of the Boxer movement might be summarized in Jung Lu's words, "China did worse than she knew."

After two years of wandering in far western provinces, Tzu Hsi returned home to her capital. It was spring, and the soft grey buildings of the native city were half-hidden in lilacs as the imperial train pulled into the station. A long file of baggage cars behind the official yellow coaches were filled with bales of silk, furs, jade, bullion—tribute collected during the court's long exile. As the empress descended to the platform, wearing a gown of imperial yellow, brocaded in the wisteria vine and richly embroidered in pearls, the air was clamorous with all the bells and gongs in the city, while a throng of nobles and high officials fell to their knees in a resounding kowtow.

Coolies had spread a carpet of damp golden sand from the station to the imperial palace, filling the ruts made by foreign gun carriages as carefully as though they were effacing deep wounds. And as the empress's cortege, flying the imperial standard with the five-clawed dragon, swept toward the gates of the Forbidden City, hundreds of loyal bannermen knelt to either side of the street.

Suddenly the palanquin of yellow satin, flashing with gold, and supported by sixteen bearers, halted before Ch'ien Men gate. The empress stepped from her chair to burn incense and recite prayers for her safe home-coming before a little shrine against the wall. Overhead, in a gutted tower of the smoke-blackened ramparts, most of the foreigners in Peking had gathered for a forbidden glimpse of the imperial party.

Glancing up, the empress saw their eager faces. Eunuchs tried to pursuade her to shield herself from this impertinent staring, but she refused. Standing in full view of the throng on the wall, she looked up and, lifting her closed hands under her chin, made a series of little bows. It was her first gesture of reconciliation toward the white-faced barbarians who had desecrated her capital, and from all along the wall came a spontaneous, grateful burst of applause.

Once the cortege reached the sanctuary of the Forbidden City, the triumph of the empress's return quickly faded. The golden sands could no longer cover the foreigners' devastation. The flower-beds were overgrown with weeds—only the common hollyhock was rampant everywhere—the marble pools silted, the pavilions emptied of their treasures; ornaments had been broken or carried off from the balustrades, even the yellow tiles stripped from the roofs.

Relentlessly Tzu Hsi made a tour of inspection of the palaces and the grounds, a throng of ladies-in-waiting, eunuchs, and officials at her back, tears flowing down their cheeks as they wrung their hands over the evidences of the barbarian's vandalism. Even the throne

213

of the Son-of-Heaven had been used as a barber's chair!

The empress finally stopped to rest in her favorite bamboo summer house. As her weeping senior advisors knelt in a circle about her chair, she turned to her chief eunuch who alone remained upright.

"Li Lien Ying," she exclaimed, "bring the rattan tea boxes from the baggage carts." Instantly he relayed the order to a half-dozen assistants who rushed off to the outer courtyard.

In her impatience Tzu Hsi rose. "Send couriers at once to tell the provinces in the Empire," she commanded. "We shall need an army of the most skilled masons, carpenters, painters, to rebuild the Forbidden City."

But the order was so shocking to the chief eunuch that his snake-like eyes emerged from their habitual retirement, and his mouth fell ajar. Camouflaging her pleasure at his amazement, the empress spoke sharply. "How dare you stand gaping? Hear and obey!"

"The Imperial Treasury is empty, Old Buddha," he said gently. "The barbarian overlooked nothing. He even dropped fishing poles into the wells and pulled up our secret bundles of pearls and precious jade."

But Tzu Hsi, observing the winding approach of a file of eunuchs bowed down by gigantic boxes, said enigmatically, "Wait and see." As the sweating, groaning eunuchs deposited their burdens on the floor of the summer house, the empress commanded, "Open the boxes!"

Without rising, the mandarins and officials edged nearer the mysterious objects on their knees, looking on while the rattan was torn loose. To a chorus of shrill cries and outbursts of incredulity, gigantic cylinders of silver, shaped like round cheeses, emerged from the wrappings.

"My lords," exclaimed the empress with a triumphant smile, "my silver cheeses!"

Bending down, Li Lien Ying tapped one of the cylinders. "It is truly silver," he announced.

Then in answer to the circle of upturned, questioning faces, Tzu Hsi said, "In the royal park at Mukden are many forgotten, dried-up wells. Long ago, I ordered a mud furnace to be built at the edge of each well. As my wealth increased, I sent cart-loads of silver ingots to be melted and poured down the wells until they were full to the curb with pure metal. Then, the walls were cemented over against thievery. I foresaw that upon my return from exile, my pantry would be empty, so I journeyed to Mukden and collected my silver cheeses that my court should not go hungry."

Li Lien Ying dropped to his knees. "Wonderful is Old Buddha!" he cried, while kowtowing. "Old Buddha leaves nothing to chance!"

The mandarins and officials thudded their heads on the floor, echoing loudly, "Wonderful is Old Buddha! Old Buddha and her silver cheeses!"

In the closing years of her life, the empress exhibited the greatest statecraft of her long reign. She had always stood for the old philosophy, the old aloofness, the old disdain. Now she made a complete about-face. Having failed in her efforts to drive the foreigner into the sea, she exerted herself to conciliate him at every turn. Her edicts of reform were issued with swift strokes of the vermilion pencil. She disbanded obsolete Manchu garrisons, abolished medieval forms of punishment and torture to force confessions from prisoners, suppressed the growing of opium, and established primary schools in abandoned Buddhist temples throughout China.

Most startling of all, in 1908 she promised the empire a constitutional form of government within one year, and expressed the hope that she might live to see the convening of the first Chinese Parliament. But this overhauling of the machinery of government came too late. The dynasty was tottering. Only Tzu Hsi's indomitable will, and the reverence in which she was held by the great mass of her subjects, prevented its collapse.

Despite her failing health, she refused to delegate authority, attending personally to the most minute affairs of state, and persisting in the rigorous schedule of rising while it was still dark for the audience at dawn. Then, early in November of 1908, she went for a water picnic on the lake in the Forbidden City, and caught a severe chill. For supper she had one of her favorite dishes, a mixture of clotted cream and crab apples which brought a return of a dysenteric complaint.

That night a court physician was summoned. His medical training had been handed down from the T'ang Dynasty (618-907 A.D.). He entered the empress's chamber on his knees and crossed the floor to her bed in this position. While keeping his eyes downcast, he was permitted to place the flat of his hand first on one side of her wrist, and then the other. This was the extent of the examination. He then withdrew to discuss her symptoms with the Grand Council.

But Old Buddha did not wait for his diagnosis. She died at daybreak, at the age of seventy-four, surrounded by the princes and officials of her realm. Her last words to her four grand councilors were significant. "Never again make a woman regent and ruler of China."

On November 9, the remains of the empress departed for the imperial mausoleum situated in a dense pine forest in the Eastern Hills, ninety miles from Peking. The funeral cortege, which traveled over a yellow-sanded road, had all the colors of a gorgeous sunset, countless mourners following under yellow silk umbrellas.

Tzu Hsi had spent untold millions on the building of

her tomb, which surpassed in size and richness of decoration any of the burial vaults of the Pharaohs. Her huge coffin had been covered with gold leaf and sprayed with four hundred coats of lacquer so that it gave the appearance of being solid gold. Tribute sent from every province by cart and camel-load, awaited her arrival at the mausoleum, testifying to far more than a perfunctory esteem.

In a contemporary account, *The Illustrated London News* gave a partial list of the treasures crowding her coffin, including eighteen pearl images of Buddhas which were placed in her arms. One watermelon and two sweet melons of jade were laid at each of her feet as well as two hundred gems made in the shape of peaches, pears, apricots, and dates. Just before the coffin lid was lowered, an imperial lady-in-waiting added a last gift of eight galloping horses of jade.

The walls of the empress' tomb were of tremendous thickness. But twenty years after her entombment, Chinese army engineers who had been trained in foreign methods of demolition tunneled underneath the vault and broke through the floor. The grave was plundered of its entire hoard of treasures, of which the value was estimated at more than $750,000,000. The empress was stripped of her robes and left naked beside the coffin.

Her body, which was in a remarkable state of preservation, was later discovered by a few faithful eunuchs. They clothed her again, this time in a plain Manchu dress, no better than the one she had worn when she came to the emperor's court as the lowest concubine. So far as can be known, she sleeps peacefully now in her lacquered coffin, but without a single jewel.

Ataturk

ATATURK: FOUNDER OF MODERN TURKEY

by Charles E. Adelsen

*J*ust fifty years ago, on the 19th of May, 1919, a blond and blue-eyed Turkish soldier was rowed ashore from an antique coastal steamer, the *Bandierma,* to step onto the bleak shore of the Black Sea port of Samsun.

Born like Alexander, that other conqueror, in a land of warrior traditions, Macedonia, this soldier of the ice-blue eyes well remembered the taste of victory. In the dry hell of the Gallipoli Campaign of the First World War he had repulsed an enemy—the British and the Anzacs, those Australian and New Zealanders of famous bravery—first at Ariburnu and later on the front at Ananfartalar, and had kept the Dardanelles Turkish, kept the enemy out of Constantinople.

An almost theatrically handsome man, he wore the medals, the stars of military orders showered on him by the grateful Sultan Mohammed VI, well. And while his efficient work merely helped postpone disaster, it did win him the title of pasha, and the Germans had given him their Iron Cross. Glory had been brief, sweet, and he had won it fairly and well on the field of battle where once only a pocket watch, worn over his heart, had stood between him and death in the bright swift strike of an Anzac bullet.

But now he could reflect, there on the gloomy beach at Samsun, the salt wind of an angry Black Sea touching that pale cheekboned face, the pine smell in his nostrils, how quickly had come and how dissipated had been that sweet taste of victory. The Great War to end all wars was done now. Turkey's allies, the Germans, had fallen. And in the Yildiz Sarayi—the Star Palace— at Constantinople, the Padishah of all the Ottoman lands and peoples, the heir to the splendor of Süleyman the Magnificent and Mehmet the Conqueror, the man who counted among his titles that of "The Shadow of God on Earth," could only sit benumbed at the sight of a fleet of foreign warships in the Bosporus, their long guns swinging now toward the very windows of the Padishah's own apartments.

In the streets of Constantinople soldiers of the Allied armies swaggered about, their officers drinking champagne among the marble pillars of the ornate pseudo-oriental decor of the Pera Palace Hotel looking on the Golden Horn, and stylish Levantine women blew kisses to men from Sussex and Southampton from the open windows of the red and white trams clattering and sparkling their way through the avenue of society and commerce, the Grand Rue de Pera. In the cafes girls in ankle-length dresses, those proper daughters of the merchant princes of Pera, learned to sing "It's a Long Way to Tipperary" in French-, Italian-, or Greek-accented voices with the pink-cheeked young men in putties and high-collared brown military tunics.

For the Allies occupying Constantinople it was the best of times. For the Turk, sleepless in his bed and hearing the last call of the *müezzin* in the rainy night —that dolorous pious voice crying from hundreds of holy mosques—for the Turk seeing the gray streamers of spring rain sweep down the Bosporus to fall on victor and vanquished, ignominy had come to sit upon Constantinople like a foul dungheap.

Constantinople, in whose defense at the Dardanelles Turks had sacrificed, in sheer numbers, whole divisions of men, had become a carnival where the revelry of the victor mocked the scores of thousands of dead men lying in their unmarked graves out along the Straits, a carnival where the Sultan-Caliph was a less than amusing puppet dangling from the strings held by the hands of his conquerors.

The blue-eyed Macedonian Turk, Mustafa Kemal, stood on the dreary strand at Samsun in the chilly air of that northern town, with no brighter prospect before him than the inspectorate of certain Turkish forces still intact up against Turkey's isolated frontier of forbidding sea and mountain range. Whereas the Sultan had sent him once into battle, he would send him now to look after the plight of soldiers with no more battles left to fight, no more leaders ready to urge them on to other battles, other victories.

Scarcely a Turk alive would have blamed Mustafa Kemal if he had sighed once for the lost glories, and had then gone about the simple duties of riding from here to there among defeated regiments of a disgraced Sultan, smallest of small men, now, sitting on an ancient throne. One was paying the price of total defeat. Nothing, it seemed, could reverse the judgment of fate.

But something would. The soldier from Macedonia had already decided that. Mustafa Kemal had whipped this same enemy into the sea at the Dardanelles. Now he would do the impossible thing again, not in the

221

cramped theater of Gallipoli, but across the steppes and mountains of Anatolia, right down, as it came to pass, to the vineyards and orchards of Smyrna, that city of forever spring or summer, white and beautiful under the Aegean sun.

There were things supposed to be lodged in the character of the Turk, that might have, should have, dissuaded Mustafa Kemal—only later would a grateful nation call him *Atatürk*, Father of the Turks—from tilting with fate. As a Moslim he might have accepted destiny, *kismet*, with no pangs of conscience obliging him to strike back. Others shrugged at the shape of things and still could display their rows of medals with unsullied pride. The Caliph, the Sultan in another of his personifications, still held sway as nominal head of all Islam. The faith was intact, even if the empire was forever shattered, and the cohesive force of the Ottomans had never been their Turkishness, but their determined loyalty to Islam, with the Sultan-Caliph as the capstone of their unity, their God-appointed chief.

Indeed, the term *Turk* was lately used for the simple countryman, the poor peasant of the good Anatolian earth who was the raw material of the armies that fought the perennial wars up and down Europe, Asia, Africa. The Empire was *Osmanli*, or Ottoman. The aristocracy, the pasha class, the court, the Sultan-Caliph himself, all, all were Ottomans.

On the other hand Mustafa Kemal knew the West, despised certain of its corruptions, but admired openly, at times vociferously, its material progress. He saw in its nationalisms a formula of devotion that might well serve his own people. He would appeal now, while the Turks yet stood in darkness and without any light, to something older in his people than Islam, older than their fealty to the House of Osman. He would inflame their spirits as Turks.

Mustafa Kemal, sublime paradox, would now reach

westward towards the civilization that had always be-witched him, westward where European nationalism had welded the peoples of old races into modern states. At the same time he would take a great leap into a past of time and space when his people had in fact thought of themselves as Turks, a time and a place in the vast spawning ground of the Turkish race, Central Asia, where inscriptions in stone written in a Turkish alpha-bet predating the Arabic script of a later time had told lovingly of a *Turkish* sky, a *Turkish* land.

He himself had a strong spiritual affinity for the lusty expansionism, the herd-following, the season-watching, freedom-cherishing life of those first Turks, those soldiers, horse-breeders, wanderers across the face of the earth. His father, Ali Riza Bey, had been a loyal civil servant of the Ottoman state, a decent citi-zen who nevertheless remains nebulous in history, and apparently almost as vague in the recollections of his son.

Yet in an Islamic society where men ruled unques-tioned, curiously it was the spirit of Mustafa Kemal's mother, Zübeyde Hanim, that loomed huge in his early life, that followed forever somehow, even after her death, her son in a world she could scarcely compre-hend, instinctively lending him the quiet council that only mothers may give even if those sons be heroes cast in a mold of Homeric proportion and character.

The mother, like the son, was fair, her eyes blue. And there is ample reason to believe that Zübeyde Hanim's lineage was interwoven with that of those no-madic people who were both the first and the last pure Turks to come across Asia into Anatolia, those remark-able people whose descendants still inhabit the unfenced spaces of Anatolia, still rejoice in the freedom of pas-ture land and green mountaintops; men fiercely—al-most belligerently—free, women strong and open-faced, people of forest and highlands who never be-

223

came in the Constantinopolitan sense in any way at all *Osmanli*.

Zübeyde Hanim, then, must have been a spiritual link with that pre-Islamic past of the Turks—no matter her persistent piety—when women did not yet wear the veil of a later society, part Arabic, part Persian, part Byzantine, but when Turkish princesses of the blood of warrior khans led Turkish riders into battle under the wild horsetail standards of Middle Asia. Out of that far-off land had come, always and unswervingly westward, the Turkish clans, their great herds, their felt-covered wagons, their splendid light cavalry following the mythic gray wolf of campfire tales and ballads to some sensed, but yet unseen, manifest destiny on the shores of the western salt sea, the *Akdeniz* or White Sea, the Mediterranean of the Romans.

In a sense pertaining to the spirit alone, Mustafa Kemal had already reached the farther shore of Turkish destiny, calling it civilization and attaching a special meaning to the word, while his people only approached their goal from afar.

Civilization! Mustafa Kemal was obsessed with the word. How he must have bewildered the Ottoman scholars of Constantinople, how he must have confounded the practitioners of the elaborate etiquette that prevailed in Ottoman society and at the court of the Padishah with his cries of *civilization*. Were they not, with their libraries, their public baths unequaled since Roman times, their gilded domes rubbing the bellies of the clouds, civilized? Historically, even the royal pages of the Grand Turk household had been taught that there was only one way for an Ottoman gentleman to sneeze. Ottoman politesse was remarked in the observations of all the letter-writing ambassadors at the Sublime Porte. What did this Macedonian upstart know of civilization?

But all of that which the Ottoman scholars called

civilization had to do with yesterdays, centuries of yesterdays. How did civilization reach out, or down, and touch and transform the Turk—unhappy word, unhappy man—of the field or the village? The faith turned the poor Turk's head to thoughts of heaven. The state, war after war, called him to the battlefields to die.

Between wars, faithfully listening to the preachments of their *hodjas,* ten thousand or a million Mehmets would plow the hard land with a simple plow, sweat or freeze on the land according to what stern season prevailed in Anatolia, and last be buried in the good earth under a carved stone if enough coppers had been saved, under a wooden slab otherwise, or even under an upright rock roughly shaped. Civilization meant more than war and prayers, Mustafa Kemal knew, but to bring it to his people one more war must still be fought.

On the Black Sea coast a storm gathered, collecting its lightning, storing up its ominous thunder. The storm was Mustafa Kemal, and the fury of that storm would not be spent until, raging over steppe land and valley, up mountains and down, it had purged the old land of its invaders. Many, the best, stood with Mustafa Kemal when he organized the Turkish Nationalist party and began to form his army in that May of 1919 while on his mission to East Anatolia.

On May 15, 1919, a Greek army had landed at Smyrna—under the protection of the Allies—with the explicit intention of detaching the western provinces of Anatolia from Turkish rule. The presence of a once-subject people on Turkish soil was more than patriotic Turks would endure and Mustafa Kemal quickly moved to take advantage of their aroused mood.

He convoked nationalist congresses at Erzerum in July and at Sivas in September which produced a national pact that demanded the preservation of Turkey's national independence and territorial integrity. The resistance groups also vowed armed resistance against the occupying forces. While Mustafa Kemal was nominally the Sultan's agent, assigned to oversee the demobilization of the remnants of Ottoman forces in eastern Turkey, he saw his own purpose clearly—he would lead Turkey to independence. A storm would roll over the invaders and he would be its center.

But not all Turks supported Mustafa Kemal's drive for independence. The Sultan-Caliph, who was in the hands of the Allies in Constantinople, outlawed the Nationalist party and sent an army uttering pious proclamations against the godless man who would not heed his monarch, who wanted only the blessings of peace— at whatever the cost in dignity—for his people. And to appease the Allies, of course. A special tribunal was convened in Constantinople and passed a death sentence on Mustafa Kemal and his lieutenants. When the Sultan was forced by the Allies to sign the humiliating Treaty of Sèvres on August 10, 1920, the die was cast; the final break was made.

The storm rolled over the land. Where there were no wagons to transport artillery shells to the front lines women of the village and the field lifted the bombs to their shoulders and walked under the blazing sun or through snowfields to where the guns stood at the edge of battle. The guns were manned by rough patriots who called themselves lion or ram, terms of brave comradeship, as they pulled forward the guns where there were no roads, fixed bayonets and charged when there were no more bullets. Later Churchill was to say of them, ". . . among the stern hills and valleys of 'the Turkish homelands' in Anatolia, there dwelt that company of poor men . . . and their bivouac fires of this moment sat in the rags of a refugee the august Spirit of Fair Play."

Mustafa Kemal retook Kars and Ardahan from Armenia in 1920—with the tacit consent of Soviet Russia.

Then, taking advantage of the disagreements among the Allies, he expelled the Greeks from Anatolia in a brilliant campaign (1921-22). Britain, France, and Italy withdrew their troops after only token resistance.

Mustafa Kemal led his "company of poor men" down off the steppes and the mountains to the shining city on the Aegean, Smyrna and celebrated with them over a victory of more precious value than they could yet understand. To them it meant home again, the Star and Crescent up once more on the masts.

Yet Smyrna was not an end for Mustafa Kemal, but a beginning. He told his exhausted, if jubilant, people, "After three years of struggle we shall continue with our endeavors, but these will now be in the fields of science, education and national economy. I am certain that we shall succeed here too: we shall become industrialists, we shall become artists. From now on let us devote our thoughts to this alone."

Civilization, the civilization of the West, was his aim and nothing was sacred or untouchable to him as he marched his way to that promised land that would mean all good things to his people. Ruthless, though in no psychological sense cruel, he bent or broke men and institutions as he went forward. Sultan and the holy office of Caliph alike he threw out as so much excess baggage. He made war on the religious establishment: "The Dervish monasteries want to make ecstatic fools of the people, but the people have decided not to become ecstatic fools."

The people had, of course, decided nothing of the sort, but Mustafa Kemal made his people participants in his dream, and at last whatever was known as his cause became their cause, too. He tore up the Arabic alphabet (the Turks, like their ethnic cousins from Central Asia, the Hungarians and the Bulgars, had never been Arabs anyway) and gave them new letters borrowed from the Latin alphabet of the West: easier to learn, easier to write, another link with the West, with civilization.

The whole monarchy he tore down, and built a Republic in its place. Women would vote in that Republic, wear no veil, and would hold public office. And no man could take more than a single woman to him as his wife. The institution of the harem was dead.

Atatürk—call him that now, as his people named him, as the world has called him ever since—was a revolutionary, but no destroyer. He tore down, but in order to build. Always before his gaze there moved the shape of that which always enchanted his energies, guided his terrible courage: the flame of civilization.

Many must have been the times when, in a life whose road was paved with ironies, he would contemplate the supreme irony of having first displayed his genius fighting at Gallipoli against men whose life was the embodiment of that civilization that he worshiped, the ultimate irony of grasping independence only after throwing into the sea at Smyrna the regiments of that nation —itself historically so brave—that first rocked the cradle of democracy. His sense of historic perspective was matchless. At Smyrna, when invited to tread upon the Greek flag, he would damn the thought of so vile a thing, saying in utter sincerity, "That is the symbol of a country's independence." He was a realist.

As a man, Atatürk was alone rather than lonely. He delighted—how famously and notoriously—in the company of beautiful women, but would not remain married to the forceful and intellectual Latife Hanim, an extraordinary woman whose dynamism sought to match his own. He could dominate parliamentarians as a lion might dominate the blasting flock, but his fascination with this power was not constant or obsessive; he would seek the solace of his farm where, alone as he could ever be, he engaged in what can only be called a devotional communion with the soil and with the

228

things that grew new and green from it.

He never demanded love from his people but only—his own stern admonition—that they work, be proud, be confident. But he was loved, especially by those of simple heart for whom he had created an entirely new definition of the word "gentleman": again and again he would call the rough, unlettered, and honest Anatolian peasant the only "gentleman of Turkey."

When Atatürk died of cirrhosis of the liver at the age of fifty-seven in a relatively simple room of Istanbul's Domabahce Palace at exactly 9:05 on the morning of the 10th of November, 1938, a flame went out and the darkness of tremendous sorrow rushed in to engulf his people. But the flame had not altogether died. Atatürk, the man, despised the veneration of the past for tradition's sake. The civilization that he built was a thing for now and for many tomorrows. Once he had contemplated how all men must perish physically, how man could only find happiness in building for those who would come after.

At the Anit Kabir, the great mausoleum where Atatürk is buried in Ankara, there are no statues of old heroes or dead statesmen. There is not even any statue of Atatürk himself. But the scores of thousands of Turks who in snow or in sunlight walk the long esplanade to his tomb may see themselves represented there in stone: the soldier, the student, the herdsman of the Anatolian soil.

Atatürk has said, "We receive our inspiration not from heaven but from life. We are guided by the Turkish nation from which we have sprung, and by the conclusions which we draw from the tragic pages of the history of the world." His inspiration was life, his goal was civilization. He lived his life well, and he lived it long enough to build the foundations of the civilization of which he had dreamed.

Marshal Mannerheim

FINLAND'S
WINTER WAR

By Ake Sandler

*O*n the evening of November 30, 1939, the Soviet Union attacked Finland without warning. Thus began the war which has come to be known as the Winter War. It lasted until March 13, 1940. France fell in five weeks, while Finland lasted three and a half months. Russia was a more imposing enemy of Finland than Germany was of France. Historians have marveled at the courage—*sisu*—of the Finns to absorb such incredible punishment without folding. By comparison, Denmark, with a population roughly the size of Finland, was taken "by telephone," as the saying goes, losing only a member of the king's bodyguard to the invading Nazis.

A true appraisal of the Finnish Winter War has, to this author's knowledge, never been made. For example, what caused the Finns to fight with such ferocity against such terrible odds? Why didn't they, like the

A Finnish ski patrol

Danes, in the name of common sense, lay down their weapons and sue for peace?

It is the author's intention to offer some explanations. To do that we must look at the events which immediately preceded this wanton, deliberate, and merciless attack upon a small neighbor, who only wished to live in peace with the world.

The incident that gave the Finns their first inkling of what was in store for them was a phone call placed to Finland's foreign minister, Rudolf Holsti, by one Boris Yartsov, a secret agent sent by Stalin to contact the Finnish government to discuss certain secret matters.

Yartsov did so independent of the Soviet legation in Helsinki, and its minister plenipotentiary there, Vladimir Darevyanski. Yartsov was empowered to deal with the Finnish government directly and make all necessary arrangements.

It soon developed that Stalin was worried about what Finland would do in case a world war broke out—particularly whose side Finland would take, Russia's or Germany's. Stalin did not believe Finland would remain neutral, and Yartsov said so to Holsti and other members of the Finnish government. And he was sure Finland would not take the side of the Soviet Union. In other words, Stalin was deeply suspicious about Finland's intentions.

These suspicions could be alleviated only by specific Finnish guarantees, the stocky, steely agent asserted. What were those guarantees? The Finnish government wondered. Among other things, Finland should commit itself, in case of a German attack on Finland, to resist and to ask Russia for military help. Russia also wanted to help in the defense of the Aland islands, which are located in the Baltic halfway between Helsinki and Stockholm and had great strategic value.

In return for these concessions (which amounted to an impairment of Finnish sovereignty), the Soviet

Union would be prepared to "guarantee Finland's integrity in its present borders," to provide military aids to the Finns, when the need should arise, and to sign a favorable trade agreement with Finland.

These demands were, of course, preposterous to the Finns and were rejected. But in rejecting them, the Finns knew what Stalin was planning; and when Stalin and Hitler made their pact on August 22, 1939—which made World War II inevitable—the Finns knew it would be a long, cold winter.

World War II erupted on September 1, 1939, and Hitler and Stalin broke the back of Poland in less than a month and divided the ravaged country. It was Poland's fourth partition. Then, while Hitler turned his attention to other problems, Stalin concentrated on Finland. The Baltic states, incidentally, had by this time been wiped off the map and were rapidly being "integrated" into the Soviet society, the kind of fate the Finns feared.

On October 23, Finland's prime minister, A. K. Cajander, declared: "Finland will not become a vassal. We shall plow with guns on our shoulders."

Stalin made impossible demands on the Finnish government, which made those a year earlier by Yartsov seem mild. Now Stalin wanted parts of the Kharelian Isthmus, so that he could form a buffer zone to protect Leningrad, which he felt was exposed. And he wanted the city of Viipuri plus the island of Hanko in the Gulf of Finland. He also demanded Finnish forces be pulled back from the Russian border. The Finnish delegates sent to Moscow to negotiate with Stalin and Molotov returned home without an agreement and it was now merely a matter of time before Stalin would attack. He accused Finnish soldiers of killing Russian soldiers along the borders.

Finland was not Poland; it could not be cut down by

*Finnish Defence Forces in Autumn, 1939,
on the Carelian Isthmus*

brute force inside a month. There was the Mannerheim Line, for one thing. For another, there was Marshal Mannerheim, one of the most brilliant military tacticians in the world. Stalin underrated both. He could not imagine that the Finns could resist for very long. There were only four and a half million Finns. How many of them could be used in the defense of the fatherland? Stalin could not possibly foresee that all Finns between fourteen and sixty-four would go to war; that the entire nation would wage war against him.

Mannerheim, cautious in peace, daring in war, had urged his government not to do anything that would precipitate a war. He was—according to his *Memoirs* —willing to go further than his government in conciliating the Russians. Not to the point of endangering Finland's security, to be sure, but he was well aware of the distinct possibility of Finland having to fight Russia alone, and this idea did not appeal to him.

Mannerheim knew Finland's limitations. Vaino Tanner, one of Finland's negotiators in Moscow, records that Mannerheim was pessimistic about Finland's ability to resist without outside help. "The army's equipment," he reports Mannerheim saying, "is extremely inadequate. Ammunition might last only two weeks. War must be avoided, if possible."

Meanwhile, across the Baltic, in Sweden, the government and the people were following events in Finland with strange fascination. Finland, once ruled by Sweden, had a peculiar position in Swedish hearts. Many Finlanders were Swedish or of Swedish origin. The Swedish minority was not only substantial and politically and economically influential beyond its numbers, but it was a national problem, and many Finns viewed their Swedish compatriots with unconcealed hostility. Swedish was a second language in Finland and spoken alongside Finnish in the Finnish Parliament. It was a required subject in the schools.

The Finnish and Swedish governments had, through their foreign ministers Holsti and Sandler, sought to improve Finnish-Swedish relations by visits to each other's countries, and by stressing what they had in common culturally. In this way, and through the efforts of others, Swedish-Finnish relations gradually improved so that on the eve of World War II, they had never been better. It also helped that both nations had social-democratic administrations which viewed each other in a fraternal spirit. Yet, on both sides of the Baltic, some ill will persisted in important quarters. And the Swedish government harbored at least one member, an old-time Marxist by the name of Ernst Wigforss, who, paraphrasing Brutus, could have said: "It's not that I love Finland less but Russia more."

This attitude was not the prevailing one within the Swedish Cabinet, or in Sweden, but it was strong enough to be felt; and ultimately it became decisive in determining whether Sweden should make common cause with Finland in its struggle for survival.

Foreign Minister Rickard Sandler tried desperately to rescue what was left of his Nordic policy; his aim was to extend and expand the neutrality of Sweden, Finland, Denmark, and Norway to include all of them in a kind of "neutrality bloc." He believed and had fought for the four states taking a common stand towards the world war he saw coming, in a sort of one for all and all for one solidarity pact. In speech after speech Sandler had pleaded for this kind of "Nordic solidarity." He had systematically developed Sweden's foreign police with this in mind. To him, Finland would now be the test whether the principle of Nordic solidarity was valid.

To that end, he promoted a demonstration of solidarity by arranging for the four chiefs of state to meet in Stockholm and show the world (and especially Rus-

*The presentation of a testimonial rifle
to sharpshooter Simo Hayha*

sia) that they were united behind Finland.

Finland's President Kallio, King Haakon of Norway, King Christian of Denmark, and King Gustaf of Sweden convened in the Swedish capital with their foreign ministers displaying, outwardly, a picture of unity. But, "behind this facade of unity, practical collaboration was quietly torpedoed," as Foreign Minister Sandler observed.

Sandler staked his reputation and career on support for Finland. He was convinced Russia was bluffing. He had been to the Soviet Union, met Litvinov and Molotov, and knew the Russian leaders better than his colleagues in the Cabinet. If the Russians were bluffing, Sweden could afford to bluff, too, he argued. All Sweden need do, he tried to persuade his colleagues in the government, was to assist Finland in the defense of the Aland Islands. Such a gesture, he was sure, would call the Soviet bluff. He could not bring himself to accept that Russia would attack if she knew she would have to deal with Sweden, too.

But Sandler's colleagues in the government, with a few exceptions, feared this first step would lead to another more precipitous step, and soon Sweden might be involved in a war with Russia which it did not desire. Help to Finland was one thing. But an action that might drag Sweden into a war with the Soviet Union was something else. From this the Cabinet shunned away—and Sandler had no choice but to resign.

Prime Minister Per Albin Hansson of Sweden formed a national government and in Sandler's place appointed a career diplomat, Christian Gunther, whose chief virtue, as an editorial said, was that "he was not Sandler."

The Soviet Union, for its part, had worked strenuously through its able ambassador in Stockholm, Madame Alexandra Kollontay, to dissuade Sweden from making Finland's case her own. How successful she was is hard to determine, but Sweden limited its help

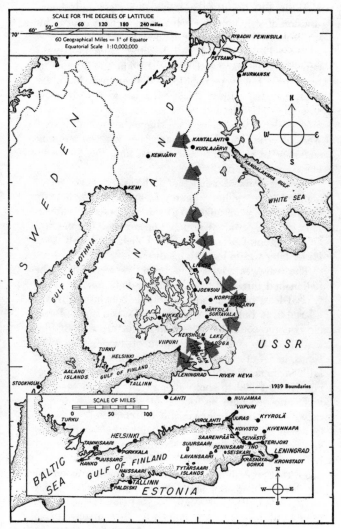

Points of Russian Invasion

once the war began to modest military aid and about a division of volunteers. It was not enough, of course, but it was more than any other nation furnished.

Finland's old friend and booster, Germany, maintained a strict hands-off policy. Britain and France offered help but were unable to deliver, principally because Sweden refused to let French and British troops and arms pass through Sweden. So, practically speaking, Finland was alone, as Mannerheim had feared. And now, at an advanced age, he was the supreme commander of the Finnish troops, and the Finns expected a miracle of their hero.

In some ways Marshal Mannerheim reminded one of another great military figure, Douglas MacArthur. In bearing they were alike. With his moustache, Mannerheim had a certain German appearance. But he was anything but Germanic in his beliefs and values—as Hitler later was to learn to his dismay.

The war was now Mannerheim's responsibility. The nation had turned it over to him to fight and, if not to win, at least bring it to an honorable conclusion. It was a large task. But the austere general was a match for it. No country could have been more fortunate than Finland to have at its helm a man of such genius. The Finns had faith in him and, more important, he had faith in them. He showed that time again—a phenomenon Hitler failed to comprehend. Later, when Mannerheim opposed him, he found out what Finnish democracy could accomplish against Nazi tyranny.

When Stalin attacked Finland the world was shocked. The League of Nations convened and expelled the Soviet Union. And President Roosevelt asked that an embargo be placed on American goods to the Soviet Union. But Stalin answered by setting up his own government in Finland, headed by a Finnish Stalinist by the name of Kuusinen, who had, maybe, a few thousand followers. But to Stalin his government was the only "representative" government of the Finnish people. He would deal with no other.

He bombed Finland from the air. His lieutenant and one of his leading heirs, Andrei Zhdanov, sent a police division from Leningrad to seize the territories Stalin had demanded from the Finns—Viipuri, Hanko, and the Karelian Isthmus. Instead this Zhdanov division was destroyed to the last man.

Zhdanov, a novice at military affairs, believing it was a mere matter of occupying certain designated areas, dispatched his men (about twenty thousand) across the peninsula. They were armed only with police weapons thinking they were on police duty. Mannerheim let them cross the small lake, then surrounded them and had his men cut them down to the last man—to "teach them a lesson." This, in turn, shocked Stalin so much that he ordered his elite troops from the Moscow District to the Finnish front.

But Mannerheim and his men held them off—even the best Russia could throw at him. For ten weeks he held the Red army at bay—an incredible achievement. So impressive was the Finnish performance that Hitler concluded—wrongly—that the Russians were push-overs, which influenced him to revise his war plans and decide, a year later, on Operation Barbarossa—the invasion of Russia.

At Suomussalmi, on the Karelian Isthmus, the fighting was particularly bitter, and the Russians sustained enormous losses—about ten Russians for every Finn. Young Finnish soldiers and officers, operating alone on skis, wrought havoc among Russian troops by single-handedly killing thousands of crack Soviet troops. One young Finnish lieutenant, Therin Aari, alone, was responsible for the death of about a thousand Russians, and Stalin placed a price on his head. It was rumored to be a million rubles!

The Finnish officer was later interviewed by foreign

Sketch of a Finnish wood after the Winter War

correspondents (including this writer) at Hotel Kamp in Helsinki. The government retired him at the age of twenty-three, awarded him the highest Finnish war decoration, the Mannerheim Cross, and let him go to Sweden, where he took a job as—a book clerk.

But all this prowess of the Finnish armed forces, individually as well as together, was to no avail. For aid was not arriving from abroad in sufficient quantities. Sweden was unwilling to provide what Finland needed. Mannerheim wrote to Rickard Sandler, who by then, in early March, had become his country's counter-espionage chief, and asked for help.

The letter was brief and to the point. The Finnish commander-in-chief asked for so many tanks, so many canons, guns, and so much ammunition. Unfortunately, there was little Sandler could do at this late date. The war was practically over. The Finns would have to accept armistice terms any time. Their losses had been enormous. Something like four hundred thousand casualties—one tenth of the population—half of them mortalities.

Why did the Finns fight at all against such odds? There are several explanations.

The Finnish government honestly believed the Swedish government would do more—a lot more—than they did. Maybe they had been misled. Maybe they had set their hopes on Nordic solidarity too high. Maybe they thought Sandler's policy—and his position —was more firmly anchored in the Swedish conscience than it was. Maybe the Swedes did not really believe that "The people of Finland might be forced to leave their own country and settle in Sweden" as Sandler told the Swedish Parliament January 17, 1940. Maybe they doubted that Finland would share the fate of the Baltic States and become "Bolshevized."

The Finns thought that although Sweden would not provide the military help Finland requested, at least it

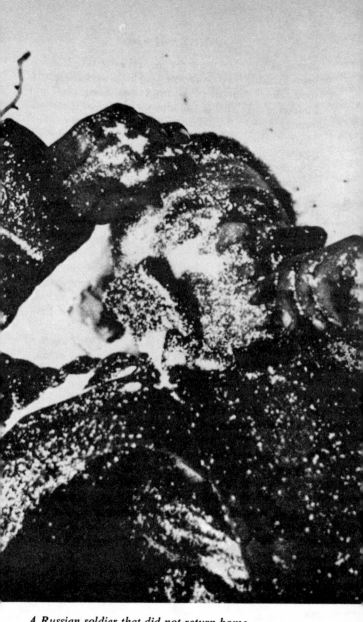

A Russian soldier that did not return home

would allow others to come to Finland's aid. Mannerheim found it hard to accept Sweden's unyielding attitude. He was shocked to learn that Stockholm told London and Paris that any attempt to "force" their way through Sweden would be resisted with "armed might," Swedish railroads would be rendered useless, electric power would be shut off, roads would be blocked, etc.

So determined was the Swedish government to keep outsiders from meddling in the Finnish Winter War that one suspects they wanted it cut short; and the strenuous efforts of Foreign Minister Christian Gunther of Sweden, in collaboration with Ambassador Alexandra Kollontay, to end the war quickly suggests Sweden was afraid the war might be going too well for the Finns, which would complicate Swedish neutrality.

So well did the Finns, under the magnificent leadership of Mannerheim, that historians might conclude that, had they received outside help, they might have defeated Russia—or at least forced the Soviet Union to give up the war as fruitless, pretty much as America now is being forced to give up the war in Vietnam. Sweden made sure no such help was possible—thereby shortening the war—all in the interest of Swedish neutrality, by which everything was judged in Sweden.

Sandlers's warning to his people that Russia had ambitions to become an Atlantic power by pushing across northern Finland seemed to come true when Molotov bluntly made new demands on Finland and asked for Kuusamo and Salla, two remote and poor forest areas which "could have no conceivable importance to the Soviet Union except as forward bases for a westward thrust," as Max Jacobson, Finland's Ambassador to the United Nations, points out in *The Diplomacy of the Winter War* (Harvard, 1961).

When he learned of these demands Foreign Minister Christian Guenther of Sweden was shocked and told Soviet Ambassador Alexandra Kollontay that Sweden

Russian grave in Finland

might have to revise her attitude—implying, in Jacobson's words, that Sweden might yet take up arms—for the sake of Suusamo and Salla, if not for Viipuri and Sortavala.

Sweden would go to war at its conclusion because now, at last, *she* felt threatened, but not at its beginning when only Finland was threatened. A more cynical position is hard to imagine. But, of course, it was an empty gesture. Russia got what she wanted, Finland had to give in, and Sweden kept quiet.

It was for this reason former Foreign Minister Rickard Sandler could speak of "national shame" and that "when the test came we were not ready" and that there had been a breakdown in the front of solidarity and that "Finland was left fighting alone." But this was rhetoric and delivered after the fact. It was too late to do anything.

Almost every Finnish home had lost a son or received an amputee, when the war was over. The destruction had been nation-wide. Towns and villages near the Russian front had been wiped out. There were thousands upon thousands of war orphans. To atone for her failure to support Finland, Sweden accepted a large number of these orphans. Sandler's wife organized Centrala Finlandshjalpen, which provided homes in Sweden for several thousand Finnish children. It was a small gesture, but it helped to restore, in some measure, the strained relations between the two countries after the war.

But these relations never became quite what they were when Sandler and Holsti were Foreign Ministers and there was high hope for Nordic solidarity.

As the son of Rickard Sandler, I was close to where the action was. But, also, as a foreign correspondent I had an opportunity to see for myself.

There is no doubt in my mind, even as I write this in early 1970, that the Finnish Winter War could have been avoided if Sweden had fulfilled its moral pledge and stood with Finland, when Stalin made his first "chess move." My father knew the Russians intimately in their capacity as Russian citizens as well as Communists. As the translator of Karl Marx's *Das Kapital,* he was viewed with some respect by Litvinov and Molotov, and even more so by the minor Soviet officials who were always present.

These small-time Communist bureaucrats asked my father if it were not possible "to construct a Soviet socialist society using *Das Kapital* as an architect's blueprint." Their naivete defied belief. And their concept of the world, including their immediate neighbors, was a caricature. This made them dangerous—especially since they believed they could bluff their way in the world and get away with it.

But when they ran up against an army more professional than their own, they were confused. Stalin was dumbfounded, according to reports, by the determination and toughness of the Finns. He is supposed to have considered whether or not he had made a mistake. In that situation Swedish support might have discouraged him from continuing.

For me, it is to admit that when the moment of truth came, Sweden lost her nerve. One member of the Swedish Cabinet confessed in his memoirs that "courage was lacking."

All nations, of course, to some extent refuse to face the truth about themselves—until so much time has passed that it can be done safely. Germany today, and the way Germans treat Hitler's thousand-year reich, is a case in point. The Russian people have yet to learn about the crimes of Stalin. So Sweden is no exception.

But the example of Finland is a reminder of the importance of courage in history. For Russia today respects Finland as it respects no other neighbor!

Each new issue of Mankind magazine brings you the delight of discovering fresh, bold, unexpected ideas relating to man's adventure on earth. You may join the Knights Templars crusading to free the Holy Land in one article, then thrill to Lord Byron's vision of the glory that was Greece in another. You could visit with Catherine the Great of Russia, travel in the western badlands with Jesse James, explore the London slums of Hogarth's England or battle with Grant at Vicksburg. The writing is lively. The subjects fascinating. The format bold and dynamic. Priceless photographs, authentic maps and drawings and magnificent art in full color illustrate articles written by the world's foremost historians and authors. Mankind is the most entertaining and rewarding magazine you and your family can read. Discover the pleasure of reading Mankind now. Your introductory subscription rate is only $5 for the full 6-issue year.

GREAT ADVENTURES OF HISTORY

These books, produced in the image of Mankind magazine, provided inter-
esting reading on a variety of fascinating subjects grouped to a singular
theme in each volume. You will enjoy reading all books in this series and,
in addition, find the varied subject matter, the quality production and
visual beauty make these books ideal gifts for any occasion.

CURRENT TITLES IN THIS SERIES.......$1.75 ea.
- THE ANCIENT WORLD (22-001)
- GREAT MILITARY CAMPAIGNS (22-002)
- THE AMERICAN INDIAN (22-003)
- THE HUMAN SIDE OF HISTORY (22-004)

GIFT BOXED SET OF ALL 4 VOLUMES.......$6.95
- ALL 4 BOOKS GIFT BOXED (22-005)